The Education System is Broken

The Education System is Broken

Strategies to Rebuilding Hope, Lives, and Futures

Cathy S. Tooley

ROWMAN & LITTLEFIELD
Lanham • Boulder • New York • London

Published by Rowman & Littlefield
A wholly owned subsidiary of The Rowman & Littlefield Publishing Group, Inc.
4501 Forbes Boulevard, Suite 200, Lanham, Maryland 20706
www.rowman.com

Unit A, Whitacre Mews, 26-34 Stannary Street, London SE11 4AB

British Library Cataloguing in Publication Information Available

Library of Congress Cataloging-in-Publication Data

Names: Tooley, Cathy S., author.
Title: The education system is broken : strategies to rebuilding hope, lives, and futures / Cathy S. Tooley.
Description: Lanham, Maryland : Rowman & Littlefield, 2016.
Identifiers: LCCN 2015046617| ISBN 9781475827385 (cloth : alk. paper) | ISBN 9781475827392 (pbk. : alk. paper) | ISBN 9781475827408 (electronic)
Subjects: LCSH: Educational change--United States. | School improvement programs--United States. | Teacher participation in administration--United States. | Education and state--United States. | Public schools--United States.
Classification: LCC LA217.2 .T66 2016 | DDC 370.973--dc23 LC record available at http://lccn.loc.gov/2015046617

∞ ™ The paper used in this publication meets the minimum requirements of American National Standard for Information Sciences Permanence of Paper for Printed Library Materials, ANSI/NISO Z39.48-1992.

Printed in the United States of America

Contents

Preface

Setting the Stage

> *For most all educators, as far back as they can remember in their childhood they have known that they wanted to be a teacher. The call of teaching is not something that is questioned or a field that many were unsure of entering. Although some people didn't know what they wanted to do when they grew up. That question is seldom a question for a teacher.*

I was born a teacher. Teaching was not something I came late to in life, as some do these days; it was calling me from as far back as when I began to understand the meaning of a career. I was born into a two parent, blue-collar family. I was a first-generation college graduate and the only one of my siblings to go to college. College was not a "given" for me, but something that I knew I needed to do to become a teacher. It was a means to an end for me. A "hoop" that I needed to jump through to become the teacher that I was meant to be.

Throughout school, I watched my teachers with a desire to understand how they taught and how their teaching may be similar to or different from the way that I would someday teach. I watched the manner in which they delivered instruction, the methodology used to enhance instruction, and the types of assessments they used. I would study every teacher and every class with the constant questions in my head: "Is this what I will do someday?" or "Is this 'good' teaching?"

Even as I got older, I asked my teachers what it was like to be a teacher. I wanted to know how it felt to be in front of a classroom. I was curious about what teaching students and watching students learn would be like, and how that would make me feel. I wanted to know how *they* knew that they wanted to be teachers, and when in their lives did they know? I was often patted on the head, so to speak, when, in grade school, I would tell my teachers, "I am going to teach someday." I often heard: "You are so young . . . just wait and see what you will do," or "Teaching does not pay enough; think about doing something else," or "Really, it is not what it is cracked up to be."

Yet, that negativity never made me waver. I knew I was going to be in front of my own classroom someday and that I would make a difference in students' lives, too. Despite what anyone said to me about the pay, the hours, the paperwork, the "difficulty," the parents, the politics, the laws, the Department of Education, the testing, or any other list given to me, I still never wavered. I never even questioned my choice. I just knew. How? I don't know that I can answer that. I just did.

There were no scholarships for me; as a matter of fact, I am not sure I really understood, as I do today, what they were and if I would even qualify. I barely understood the financial ramifications of going to college, and frankly, that just did not matter to me. Paying for college was not something I worried about. I just knew that I needed to go to college to be the teacher I was driven, even destined, to be.

Early on in my college career, the classes that made me the most happy and gave me the most peace were the classes that allowed me to be in a classroom in some sort of capacity. From classroom observations to working in small group settings, I knew even more that teaching was in my blood. I was at home in a classroom, and when I was in front of a class, leading a lesson or working with a small group of students to help them understand material, I felt at home.

I began my teaching career in the fall of 1984. I began by teaching high school Spanish and English at the very school where I had just completed my student teaching. *I was a teacher*, and my career had begun.

I knew in my heart that I wanted to be an administrator and run my own building, someday. I spent twenty years in the classrooms of that same school. I loved what I did, and I was good at it. I had great evaluations. I assisted several student teachers as their supervising teacher.

I was active in my school community serving on several committees and even became very involved in the teachers' union. I was respected and well-liked (I think at least) and loved what I did every day. I went to work knowing, based on my results, that I was making a difference in students' lives. I was living my dream.

I began receiving little notes and letters from students telling me what a difference I had made in their lives. I kept them all. I received countless hugs and heard over and over, "I would not be here if it weren't for you." All of those times I would reflect, thinking, "How can you put a price on making a difference in so many students' lives?" I was so honored.

I never took any of those moments for granted and felt so blessed and honored for each and every one of them. My heart remembers every story. I smile at every e-mail updating me on students' lives after high school; I follow them through the papers and reunions. Year after year, student after student, I continued to touch students' lives and, more importantly, was touched by theirs. I had a rich, full, fulfilling, wonderful life as a teacher. There was simply nothing better as a career for me.

In the fall of 2002, I began my journey toward becoming an administrator. I became an assistant principal in the fall of 2004. In the fall of 2011, I felt the itch to have a "building of my own" and left my school after twenty-seven years. I remained in my new school, as their principal, for three years, before I left public education after thirty years and took a principalship at a charter school for six months.

After thirty years in public education, the charter world was not one that I could wrap my brain around (another whole book on that topic) and was "downsized due to budget cuts" in November of my thirty-first year in education.

Remember, I did not grow up with educators in my family. I had some great teachers, but none that were the reason that I wanted to teach. Some, to the contrary, told me later in life that I was not "college material." In spite of all that, teaching was my calling and where I spent the majority of my career. I say all of this to make one thing clear about this book. Education is in my blood. It is who I am. I have spent the past thirty-plus years of my life giving my all to this career and I am proud of the difference I have made. This book in *no way* is an attack on education. Lord knows there is enough of that going around.

If you are reading this part of this book to collect "dirt" or to hear about a scorned educator's vindictive path of retribution, then I am afraid this is not your book. You should probably put this down and continue on down the shelf for another book, or, you can always listen to the media as there are plenty of stories that attack education. This book is the opposite. This is a book written from the viewpoint of an educator who has spent her life in education. Having done that, I know (just as any educator does) what is wrong with our system.

The intent of this book is to look at our educational system in its current form and to evaluate not only *why* this system is broken, but also *how* we might move forward, together, to fix it. Remember, this is a view from one educator's *multiple* lenses. After thirty-plus years in education, my experiences have allowed me a broad view of education, as seen from the classroom to the principal's office.

Those lenses have included being observed in my own classroom as a teacher, to observing many classrooms as an administrator; from receiving evaluations as a teacher, to writing many teacher evaluations as an administrator; from administering the tests to many students as a classroom teacher, to assisting many teachers in evaluating their own tests and students' data as a building-level principal.

That multiplicity of positions allowed me to handle discipline issues in my own classroom, as a teacher, and also as an assistant principal, suspending, even expelling students based on their actions. My experiences allowed me to talk and work with parents as a teacher, while their children were in my class, and as a principal, meeting with that same parent and working with their child's teacher (both positively and negatively).

The final opposing polarization was felt through my relationship with my superintendent. As a classroom teacher, there is almost an anonymity that exists between a teacher and the superintendent, who, depending on the school size, may not even know who you are, but the complete opposite becomes true once that teacher becomes an administrator. As an administrator, superintendents know every move that is made. That was such a revelation to me as I moved from the classroom to an administrative role.

Throughout my years, there are countless examples of school boards who worked to support me in my role as a teacher, and there are school boards who behaved more like overzealous stage managers micro-managing my role as a principal—a specimen under their microscope. Every educator, including me, has worked with their local department of education with a teacher's view of testing, implementation of standards, and expectations, but I have also been to the opposite side, as a principal, feeling the pressures of grading and evaluation.

My thirty-plus years of experience have allowed me to walk on both sides of a building where our students go every day, in the role of a teacher and that of an administrator. Those experiences have demonstrated to me the good, the bad, and the ugly hidden by the backdrop. They have permitted me, first-hand, to experience the pride and joy of one moment and in the next moment the pure evil of another . . . all under the mask of "what is best for kids."

Introduction

Understanding the Play That is Education

There has been study after study, research after research, attack after attack, and thought after thought to explain why our educational system is so far behind other countries'. Why are some schools failing despite all of the money, resources, and efforts that seem to be given to them? Why do teachers seem to not be teaching the necessary information that our students need to be successful? Why are our schools failing? What is happening to the educational system? How do we fix our failing schools?

These are the questions you will hear over and over on every news broadcast, in every paper, and from every media outlet imaginable, yet it is almost certain that educators are not asking these questions; they already know the answers. Not one educator is scratching his or her head asking the above questions. There is no educator right now buried under a mound of ungraded papers, searching for the newest standard for testing, who is perplexed by our current system and how to fix it. There is also no administrator questioning why our schools are in the mess they are in.

There is no educator who, if asked right now, is wondering why our students are not finding the success they deserve in our schools. The obvious question then becomes, if educators already know what is wrong with our educational system today, why aren't they fixing it? Two easy answers.

1. No one is asking them.
2. It would be political and career suicide to say what needs to be said.

The intention of this book is to pull back the curtains on the stage that is public education and share what every educator already knows, but is unable to say. Being in education for over thirty years allows a unique perspective to explain the real inner workings of schools and how the things that are reported are distorted and never really tell the entire story, leaving out the view of the educator. The intention is to reveal what is "behind the curtain" of the educational stage, so that all of us can move forward together to fix our system.

It has been said that knowledge is power, and that once we know better, we can do better. Beyond a shadow of a doubt, once we read and hear the voices of our educators we can move forward with viable solutions. After reading numerous books outlining the problems in education, I realized they are often written from an *outsider's* point of view. It has not been my experience to have read *one* that outlines what the directors on the stage, the teachers and the administrators, already know.

Additionally, none of these stories, articles, or books, that tell us what education is all about and what needs to be done to fix it, are written by people who have spent one day in front of a classroom teaching, let alone running a building. This will not be a book full of statistics, data, charts, or analysis of data. This is a book from one proud educator's heart, scripting what has been felt and known through day-to-day experience to be true. How is that truth known? From personal experience for the past thirty-plus years.

So, how do we fix our failing schools? We begin by finally taking the educator out from behind the desk being *told* what they are doing right and wrong and bring them to the table to *share* in the decisions and solutions regarding what is happening in our schools. It is time to part the curtains on our public school system and show you the villains, the heroes, the talented, and the not so talented. It is time to give you a behind the scenes view of our educational stage.

We can all learn not only what many educators still in the field are frightened to say, but what we can all learn from them. It is time to give a microphone to those who are center stage, with the volume turned way up with the spotlight shining right on them.

The goal for writing this book is to begin some true dialogues. Our society must be one that believes that our teachers, our administrators, and most importantly our students deserve the best. My father always said to me, "Never burn a bridge that you may have to re-cross." As this book pulls back the curtain on education, it is done knowing that there is a fire coming on that bridge. I may even be holding the match, so there is a comfort looking at the bridge of my career before it is burned knowing that I cannot go back once this is lit. There will be, and must be, a firestorm of truth if we are to fix our failing schools.

So, here is to looking at my career from the other side. Here is the match; here is the truth; and here is my view. Turn up the spotlight, turn on the microphone, sit back and take your seats. Here we go.

Curtain #1

Politics in Education on a Larger Scale

Education today is full of political agendas, political posturing, and political maneuvering all precariously balanced on the backs of our schools. Caught in that posturing, maneuvering, and political agendas are teachers, administrators, parents, and most importantly, our students.

Let's begin this chapter by stating that the supposedly all-wise oracle determining the fate of education lives in Washington, DC, and funnels this wisdom to state boards of education, which then funnels it to local school districts. Effectiveness in education varies from state to state and exists completely at the whim of the current political party's maneuvers and current political platforms. You see, as all educators know, whatever the political "whim" is at the time, it will be completely uprooted four years later when new politicians take power or a new political party is in the majority.

Think about that for just a moment. It is quite feasible for children to have their complete educational expectations, testing formats, lengths of school day or year, and who their teachers are, and how those teachers are evaluated change at minimum three times during their educational journey. That may not seem to be much—unless it is your child being bounced around by those political whims.

For you see, education has become a platform that politicians stand on to tout their beliefs on "what our students need" and "what is wrong with our schools today." Education has also become one of the biggest battlefields in politics today. Everything from the length of the school day or year to the evaluation of teachers to testing and what that looks like, how long it lasts, and when it occurs have become politically charged issues. They are so politically charged and have become such a platform that, too often, they have led to such political divide and dissention that no decision or progress really gets made at all.

There could be an entire book written about how our children and the topics of what they learn, how they are tested, when they are tested, and how schools operate have become a political platform on which many stand. One could also spend an entire book talking about the laws and countless edicts that have come down from Washington, DC, to the state and then to the local level of schools that are crippling learning in the classroom.

One could also talk about the childlike behaviors of so many politicians who are too busy arguing to see what the damage all of their arguing has done and is doing to our schools. Each and every state across this great nation could tell you story after sad and pathetic story about how education is in the grip of some political stalemate and is caught in the never-ending cycle of political bureaucracy.

And these edicts are coming from politicians who, other than going to school at one time themselves, have no experience running a school on a day to day basis. They have no idea what good instruction looks like. They have no experience in working with a struggling student or their family. They have no idea how to assist a successful student in finding their next path in life. They can give you their *opinions* regarding what a path should look like and they say what will ensure their being re-elected, but they have no idea how to help a student find their path in life. And they have no idea what a school, most schools, look like day in and day out as successes or failures.

Remember, most of the people who are making the decisions about schools have two things in common.

1. They are not experienced educators with any educational training or background.
2. Committees, subcommittees, and lobbyist groups are not comprised of or represented by educators.

Governmental agencies tell schools what they are going to do, but do nothing to involve the very people who will need to carry out their edicts. There was a recent example in fall 2013 in Indiana, in which the state passed a law (remember most schools have already started by then) that needed to be carried out by October of the same year. This was a law that would impact staffing, change students' schedules completely, and change what was being taught by many teachers all *after* the school year had already begun.

Educators were stunned that such an edict could happen with so little regard to the ramifications for them. Meetings were held, and the end result was, "Make it happen. You deal with it." That is just one example that building-level administrators, in collaboration, were forced to live with, but there are countless others just like it across every state of this great nation. And, all this political dancing leaves teachers, students, and administrators switching partners for a dance to a tune they have not even heard yet. This is clearly not the way to run a school system.

How do we fix this political maneuvering? How do we utilize political platforms so that the many politicians who are standing on those platforms assist our schools? How can we, as a society and as parents sending our sons and daughters to schools, ensure that our voices are heard on the political stage?

This solution is so easy that it seems unfathomable to understand why it is not already happening. We have to begin to get the very people most impacted by any decision in education to be involved in those decisions. We must demand that no political decision about our schools be made without the direct input of those most impacted by and charged with carrying out the decision, the educators.

We can easily, in this technologically advanced time, at the very least, take a survey to assess the expertise of the educators most impacted by the decisions being made in Washington, DC, and at more local levels of government. We must involve teachers and administrators when looking into education and making decisions that impact instruction. The very professionals we have trained to run our schools and to teach our children must be involved in the decisions that impact their ability to do what they have been hired to do.

Curtain #2

Politics in Education on a Local Level

Education at the local level is divided between two very distinct groups of leaders: the administration and the school board. If those groups are working in sync, there is harmony; but, if there is no harmony or there is disagreement between those groups, there is division, confusion, mistrust, and a toxicity that damages schools.

This chapter spotlights the local level of school "government" to fix our broken system. If there is constant confidence that we can fix education on the local levels, see success in our classrooms, and begin a grass-roots movement supported by the very people most affected by these laws (the parents, the students, and the educators), *we will* create the change that our government will have to listen to.

If we, as those most vested in the educational system, unite against governmental, political ramblings, grand standing, and political agendas, we can rebuild our schools and fix our broken system.

So let's begin in our school. . . .

With any successful organization, from Fortune 500 companies to the smallest small business, success and measurements of success are often defined by leadership teams. The leadership in any organization is not only the beacon, but should, in successful companies, have the experience to guide the company to success.

It is that leadership team that directs the play through both smooth and rough rehearsals. It is that leadership team that runs the rehearsal over and over until the show is perfect. It is that leadership team that not only redirects a play that is floundering and not finding success but finds the source of the weakness to prevent it from happening again. It is the leadership team that, when a close of the play is coming, looks for direction to whether that closing curtain will open again.

It is that leadership team that guides the cast, assists them in both flawless and flawed shows. It is that leadership team that evaluates the value and worth of each and every person in the cast and how they can play a role in successfully unifying the entire cast. It is that leadership team that measures the day-to-day tracking of the team to determine if the show is moving toward the goal and how, if they are not, to get back on course.

It is the leadership team that builds up a team member who may be down, disciplines ones that may need discipline, encourages ones that may need encouragement, supports ones that may need support, and provides differentiated assistance that is personalized to each team member's needs. It is that leadership team that, even in the most perfect of performances, guides the cast to the next opening night.

At all times, that leadership team is aware of where we are going, how we are going to get there, and what to do once we get there to get even better. What that success is and how it is defined we will talk about in upcoming chapters, but it is safe to say that schools, just as any Fortune 500 company or any successful company, want to succeed and rely on the leadership of their schools to be successful. Schools have looked for success and have leaned on their leadership team to guide them to success for years.

In schools, the "leadership team" is made up of two key, yet very different, components:

1. Administration, in and out of the building: This includes the building-level assistant principal(s), the principal, the assistant superintendent(s), the superintendent, and a myriad of other central office or building-level directors and coaches.
2. The school board: This is composed of elected individuals from the school district.

This local leadership team is the most influential decision-making body in the day-to-day running of any building, and, more importantly, the tone of that building. Administrators and teachers alike have had experiences in buildings that are run by fear and buildings that are run with a sense of collaboration and shared leadership. Depending on how these two groups (administrators and school boards) work together can and will make a difference in what is happening in the schools that they lead. Administrators and teachers have felt, and know, when the relationship between these two groups is adversarial or contentious. They are very aware of where the divide happens and where the disparities are in this governing body.

If a school board supports their administration, teachers, too, feel supported and feel united as a team, but if the school board and the administration, any of the administration, are at odds or contentious, teachers too feel uneasy or insecure regarding their place in the classroom and the support they will receive.

Compare that relationship, if you will, to the feeling a child experiences when his or her parents are close, getting along, and are loving and respectful to each other. Contrast that to the experience the child feels when his or her parents are fighting and argumentative. Teachers feel that "fighting" too and are often pawns in the political gambits of school boards and the administration. Depending on the level of hostility, teachers' very jobs can be at stake.

What the solutions are to fixing and working with these two very different arms of the political world of schools will be addressed later, individually. Let's begin by looking at each of the groups and how they can assist in fixing our broken system.

Curtain #3

Administrators on the "Fast Track"

Let's begin with the administration both in and out of the building. Administrators, from superintendents to principals, to assistant principals and assistant superintendents, have experience in education. They, in the public school systems, have gone to school, received training, and have state-affiliated degrees permitting them to be administrators.

Each state varies in what administrators' educational requirements look like, but all states have some sort of requirement for what it takes to be an administrator in the public school system. This is only in reference to public schools, because most charter and private schools do not share that same requirement. Some administrators have a great deal of experience in the classroom before becoming administrators or superintendents, while others are on what we in education call "the fast track to administration."

Let's pause here for a moment and talk about "the fast track to administration." Educators know exactly which administrators took the "fast track to administration." This is not a difficult question for any teacher who has been teaching for more than a year. Test me. Walk into any school building right now and ask any teacher to name an administrator who took the "fast track to administration." They will smile, laugh a little, want to know why you are asking, but know what you mean and can, with very little effort, come up with a name if they are comfortable enough with you to answer. My intention here is not to bash those "fast trackers," but rather to assist you in understanding what it means and how it plays out to the success in schools.

So, what is a "fast tracker"? To understand this you have to understand that the entire concept begins with pay. As we all know, teachers in most states are not paid a high wage. No, there will not be a money debate here . . . again, another book, another chapter. No one goes into education for the money; however, in a later chapter, there will be a discussion on the cost and expectations impacting teachers, including the lack of pay. Let's just agree here for the sake of the point in this chapter, that in education the only way to make "money" is to leave the very thing that educators went to school to do . . . teach.

Let's pause here and point out the ludicrous nature of that statement. Most teachers went to college, paid good money, studied, and got a degree *to teach*. They also went to college knowing that they were going into a career that would not make them rich; yet, they felt it was their calling. They felt they could and would make a difference in children's lives.

Unfortunately, the only way to make a respectable living with the college degrees they earned is to leave the classroom. Let me make that point one more time to make it very clear. In order to make money or at least what most would consider a respectable wage in education, teachers *must* leave the very classroom they studied in school to lead. They must leave the classroom and go into administration, away from their beloved classroom. Yes, this is true. Shocking, but true. And every educator knows it.

The point here for the "fast trackers" is that, in most school districts, an administrator's pay is significantly more than a teacher's. Upon leaving the classroom *with twenty years of experience*, pay increases may rise $30,000 or more. That is not a small sum and is why some educators are on what we call the "fast track to administration." Remember, if teachers make the move to administrator earlier in their career, their raise could be significantly more.

A teacher with twenty years' experience may be doing quite well per se, and some school districts pay very well compared with many other local and surrounding school districts, but even then, to enter into administration with a $30,000 pay increase is nothing to scoff at. While that new contract will increase the amount of days required to work from a teacher's contract to an administrator's contract, make no mistake, that $30,000 raise is huge.

Just imagine for a moment, what pay difference that would be for a *young* "fast tracker" with a few years of experience. Depending on the school district and what they pay teachers as compared to the package offered to most administrators, it is easy for a "fast tracker" to receive a $30,000 to $70,000 jump in pay in one move. That makes it very easy to understand why there are so many "fast trackers" and why they do it. But, therein starts the problem.

Often those "on the fast track" have not spent enough time in the classroom to know effective strategies for teaching for which they are now going to have to evaluate teachers. They themselves may or may not have experienced enough time in the classroom to be able to assist a teacher in being better at their craft. There are teachers evaluated by administrators who have spent as little as three to five years in the classroom.

Regardless of the willingness then (and now) to learn and grow from another person's perspective on how to make the classroom better and how to assist students in growing, the dilemma and lack of experience of many "fast trackers" finds experienced teachers asking questions of the younger, less-experienced administrators and hearing statements such as, "Come on, you have been doing this longer than me. You could probably teach me a thing or two." Or, a personal favorite was when a teacher, who was being observed by a "fast tracker" administrator, was sent to a senior teacher for advice because the administrator did not really have any suggestions.

There are a myriad of frustrations for administrators upon discovering that their wheelhouse of knowledge is just not sufficient to assist a veteran teacher, who was not in any form of trouble in the classroom, to continue to get better. That is not an attack; it is just fact. There is something to be said for first getting experience in the field in which you want to lead.

Now please, make no mistake here, this is not an age issue . . . it is an experience issue; one that is easily solved. There have been many "fast trackers" who, after many years in education, get better at being administrators, but they do so often on the backs of good teachers. They lean on the good teachers to "administratively" assist other teachers in getting better.

Many "fast trackers" are *great* building managers and can keep the boat afloat with no problem. They have no issues working with the maintenance department. They can resolve the pep session schedule that seems to be bothering everyone. They can work with the cafeteria to solve a myriad of issues, and they are willing and usually open learners. They are just lacking that experience *in* the classroom to be the strong educational leaders that are so critical in our schools today.

In many states, there is no minimum requirement on how long teachers must *teach* before they can become administrators. It is not unusual for an educator with about fifteen years of experience to have a principal with seven years of experience with only three of those years *in* the classroom. A superintendent may have a total of ten years' experience (in the classroom, as a building principal, and now a superintendent) never having any experience in the running of a high school as all of his experience was in an elementary school and may be at a loss most of the time as to how to support a high school teacher.

In most cases, administration does what it knows and gives what it can, but since their gas can of experience was never filled past a quarter of a tank, you cannot expect to get a full tank worth of experience from them. These "fast trackers" are good people with good intentions and will get their feathers ruffled at this part of the book. This is *not* an attack on them as a *person.*

For educators there is an understanding why "fast tracking" happens. Educators know what it is like to live on a teacher's salary for twenty years while raising three children. They understand how much time it takes to be a good teacher and that even more time is required to be a good administrator. Therefore, if what education needs is true instructional leaders, these educators must have the *experience* necessary to be able to lead.

Consider this analogy: If there were a choice between taking a car to a mechanic who had thirty years of experience and a mechanic with two years of experience, the choice would be obvious. That is not an attack on inexperienced mechanics, as certainly, in time, with proper guidance and learning, they will be wonderful mechanics, but they need that time and experience. With all of that being said, is there a magic amount of time an administrator should spend in a classroom before they are "right" to leave and become an administrator? No—for we must allow for natural talent as well. What must be considered in choosing administrators is detailed in the following paragraphs.

There must be a minimum amount of time (however it is defined by each state, school, or district) that, before becoming administrators, an educator must be in the classroom teaching students. Not being a coach, not being an assistant, but in the classroom day after day with students. There is nothing of greater value than that time. Ask any person from any walk of life how they got good at their craft and they will tell you by doing it year after year. Teaching is no different. How do you get good? You do it, you fail at it, you try again, and you keep going. Time is the very least we can ask of our educational leadership.

Being mentored by a more experienced, same-level administrator should at least be required of all upcoming administrators. When taking over that first building as a principal, it is most effective and makes the biggest impact on students if there is a mentor who has more experience in being a principal at that same level.

That difference would be simply unimaginable to most new administrators. That difference would not only allow them to make their own personal lives better, but would also allow them to have even more impact and meaning on their staff and their students. There is certainly some learned information from being an assistant principal, but there certainly is a lack of preparation regarding what is required in order to be the educational leader, the principal, which any successful building needs.

Due to the lack of any form of mentor, buildings are not getting the educational leader they deserve, and remember some new leaders have had many years of experience in education. Imagine how those leaders with far less experience feel. Even with experience at the very school where their teaching career began, the first day of school as an assistant principal is still one that will be remembered forever.

Here is one example.

The bell rang, all the students ran to their classes, and the teachers closed their doors to start that first day of school. The new administrator stands in a long hallway that, once full of students, is now all but empty except for that random student running late to the classroom he could not find. The new administrator thinks, "Now what?" What does an assistant principal do now? Where is one supposed to go? What is one supposed to do?

Experience has taken them from this time last year as a veteran classroom teacher knowing exactly what to do and when to do it in the classroom to now, as an assistant principal, wondering what to do with the day. So, with that lack of knowledge as to what to do, and that empty hallway in front of them, they walk back to their empty office, sit in their chair and think, "Well, administrator, with that license . . . now what?"

Then in walks that first student who got in trouble and was being sent out of class (yes, first day, and first period). Contemplating the referral the teacher has written, the new administrator has no clue as to what to do. There is no mentor. There is no direction. There is no state standard or standardized test by which to measure this referral.

Remember, this is a child (okay, well young adult), and an administrator needs to handle this right. Experience, as a classroom teacher, cannot be relied upon in this moment as a guide on how to deal with this discipline issue now staring them in the face. At the same time, that experience is also frustrating, because, as a former teacher, the administrator would never have referred a student to the principal for this infraction, especially on the first day of school.

But, none of that matters. All that matters now is this referral written from a teacher (who last year was probably a colleague), and this student who has done something that another classroom teacher felt needs to be disciplined. As an assistant principal, the determination must be made about what to do with this student with no history, no experience, no guidance, and no mentor. Remember, this incident was not witnessed by the administrator; there is no history on the administrator's part regarding this student and this teacher, and there is a complete lack of understanding on how, on the first day of school, the student is standing here in the office.

So, what is one to do? There is a digging deep inside of the administrator and a reliance on three things: expertise with disciplinary issues during her time as a teacher, her experience as a parent, and the experience of an administrator right across the hallway. Logic walks the new administrator across the hall, experience looks him straight in the face, and the new administrator asks, "What is one supposed to do with this?" The experienced administrator laughs and walks the new administrator through the process.

That was the beginning of what must have been a million questions that were asked of her by the first year administrator, and it must have taken an exorbitant amount of time from his day, but that is how the process, the solutions, the discipline, and the behaviors are conveyed. That help and time received from the experienced administrator that first year came out of the kindness of his heart, but not because our system put that in place. Doesn't that seem odd?

That power, as an assistant principal, to suspend, even expel students from their education, is given with no guidance, no support, no mentor, or any manner in which to be successful. And, remember, sometimes an administrator taught in that same building for twenty years, so they were already familiar with the day-to-day protocols and paperwork. Imagine what a "fast tracker" would experience.

To become a teacher, it was a requirement to spend ten weeks in a classroom teaching with a mentoring teacher watching and guiding every move very closely. The colleges pay supervising teachers a small stipend for the time and efforts they take to guide and mentor, yet, as the transition to an administrator begins, there may be a mentor (with no pay) who can assist; however, some states have now, due to budget cuts, even eliminated that.

So rest on that fact! The "fast trackers" are having the same struggles with far less experience under their belts to support them as a teacher with many years of experience would afford them and no guidance, support, or mentor to assist.

Curtain #4

The Role of Our Administrators is Confusing

Each year, more and more emphasis is placed on administrators to become the educational leaders in their buildings and not just the managers. Yet, what ends up happening is that the "management" side of running a building is still necessary so the educational leadership portion is often put on the back burner.

It is tough to think about, as a building-level leader, how to promote the use of technology in your classrooms when the school secretary quit and you need to hire another one. Or, it is challenging, as a building-level leader, to balance yet another parent calling to state that someone was mean to her at the ball game the other night, or the custodians want to know what student has written on the bathroom stalls for the third time this week, or the math teacher wants to know why you had the mandatory monthly fire drill during his fourth-period calculus class again, or how you are going to deal with the fact that you are running out of file folders to keep the permanent student files and have no money in the budget to add more, all while looking to "lead" your building.

This thought could go on and on, but let me make the following point: leadership in our schools today is made up of well-intentioned, educated, and mostly experienced individuals who are trying to manage and lead a ship at the same time.

There was an old analogy that fits best what is happening in our schools to administrators every day. Good administrators are flying the plane with a huge hole in it and repairing the hole while the plane is flying. That about sums it up. Every administrator knows that to have a truly successful building one must focus on leading that building, not managing it. Every good administrator would agree with that statement, then take a look at their daily tasks, and laugh at what *needs* to be done in comparison to what *will* be done.

Every administrator knows that student success is important, but that the fire in the restroom is urgent. So, too often what unfortunately ends up happening is that administrators' days are consumed by the things that are urgent causing the things that are important to be pushed aside and often neglected.

As an administrator it becomes important to compartmentalize the day. Logic has them dealing with people (staff and students) while they are in the building and dealing with e-mails, paperwork, and returning calls after everyone had gone home. They end up working twelve- to fourteen-hour days (plus countless Saturdays). That is not a complaint here, though there will be those who say, "You make a good salary so quit your complaining."

In response to that statement, remember there are only twenty-four hours in a day, seven days in a week, and fifty-two weeks in a year. Any administrator is still human. Many of them are mothers and fathers and have aging parents as well as children of their own. We are in education because we want to make a difference and we know we can, but after attending school all day and the countless events after school and on weekends, and dealing with the urgent, the important sometimes falls in the way of either sleep or sanity!

There are simply not enough hours in the day to "keep the plane in the air" per se, and to repair it. What far too often happens is that administrators spend their days "managing" their buildings and are left only a few precious moments or meetings to try to look at how to "lead" their buildings. This is a compromise.

Everyone would agree that the most important job of any leadership team is to spend time and effort in leading their school. Looking at data, evaluating teachers, monitoring learning in our classrooms, and making necessary adjustments based on the data should consume at least 90 percent of any administrator's day. That is true if they are to be true educational leaders. No one would disagree with that fact and most stakeholders would agree that this is what any great administrator is doing, or should be doing, every day for most of their day. If that is what you believe happens, then you would be sadly mistaken.

In reality, most administrators are spending 90 percent of their day managing their buildings. When a parent shows up unannounced, mad about one topic or another, and they demand to be seen immediately, whatever "leading" that was happening at that time stops. When a crisis happens (fight, custodial issue, time schedules, phone call, etc.) any "leading" stops. When a teacher wants to vent that her class size is too big, all leading stops. When a staff member resigns, retires, or is encouraged to leave, again, you guessed it; leading is pushed aside. Throughout the day, "leading" is interrupted by "management."

There is story after story about how great leadership meetings that are looking at data and making movement toward success are interrupted to deal with a management issue. Every educator knows what you are thinking here, well then, just don't let that happen. Tell the parent to wait? Tell the issue to hold on? Have someone else deal with it. Call someone else to handle the situation.

Again, *no one* waits to see the principal. They will, if not satisfied, leave the principal's office, go to the superintendent or the media, so just to be safe the principal will take that meeting. Or, imagine this news story, will you? Principal allows students to have a major fight in the building while the entire administrative team was in a meeting. Or, field this phone call when your daughter comes home upset because, at your encouraging as a parent, she went to see the principal today and was told the principal was in a meeting.

Every educator knows that management supersedes leadership. Every administrator knows that it is better to "put out the fire" than to let it erupt into an inferno regardless of what leadership is put on pause. No one wants the hassle, the fire, the delay, and the repercussions; therefore, leadership is interrupted.

The point is that the very thing that is so vital to the success of our schools is pushed to the wayside and not addressed. Every administrator knows that being an educational leader is their most important role. They are not shirking that role, nor do they undervalue it. There is simply not enough time, or enough resources, or the respect given to it to allow it to happen. So, what ends up happening is "good" buildings are defined as those that are managed well, and we continue on to another school year not changing much from the last one.

Parents, who are the most vocal about their schools, do not really understand what it takes to "lead" a building; therefore, they cannot understand the time necessary to do it. A question repeatedly asked by close friends might be, "What do you do all summer or during breaks when there are not students in the building?" They are so confused by what might possibly need to be done if there are no teachers or students in the building to "manage." Hysterical laughter erupts from every administrator's lips every time that question is asked. It is without question that most administrators look for and crave that time to lead their buildings. Summers and breaks become the most stressful and busiest.

We have examined the roles and the responsibility of our administrators and how the minutes of their days are being filled. We cannot claim that we, as a society, want our schools to be different, but fill the plates of our educational leaders with management tasks that keep them from what matters most. We must provide the tools, the time, and the resources to allow administrators to lead if we want to see change in our school systems. We must value management, and put those people in place to manage our buildings. We must begin to understand, respect, and value the time and the urgency of having educational leaders in our buildings by removing the management from them if we ever want to see growth in our buildings.

Curtain #5

The Political Reality of Administration

Addressing the political portion of being an administrator in any building and how vital it is to the longevity of the administrator's career must be addressed. Every decision, every movement, every day has a political cost to an administrator that is often unfair and runs great administrators out of the profession.

When first becoming an administrator (specifically a principal), a good administrator friend shared an analogy that to this day has never been forgotten. He said, "Cathy, you must understand that every decision you are now going to make as a principal will have a political cost. Think of your life as a building-level leader as having a political cup. Every decision and every choice you make will either put political sand in your cup or will take political sand out of your cup. You will remain as a building-level administrator as long as the decisions you make keep sand in your political cup. Once your political cup is empty, you are done as a principal of that building."

That concept was one that required a little mind bending and time as a building-level principal to experience it first-hand. There were some decisions that I made as a principal that made the students and the parents happy; everyone loved them. These added political sand to the cup. There were other decisions that upset some students or parents, who were vocal to the school board. These took political sand from the cup.

As time continues, building-level principals recognize contentions that arise from some of their decisions. There becomes a very clear awareness and an innate evaluation of every decision being made, to consider if that decision will add or subtract sand from the political cup. There is often an inner struggle in making some decisions, because, while knowing they are decisions made for the best of the students, there is also the knowledge that some of those same decisions will not be popular and take sand from the political cup.

As a principal, there is a constant internal struggle knowing "doing what was best for kids" could cause the political cup to empty so far that it ultimately could end up costing the job. That is the struggle for every administrator. Do they do what is right for students, or do they do what is right for their careers? Administrators have families to feed, too. That pull is being felt by every administrator and for those that have lasted for a long time, they are putting the political answer first and keeping their cups full.

The decisions that are being referenced here are not what some would even consider the "big" decisions, but rather they are the decisions that are being made each and every day by school leaders across every school system. Let me give you a couple of examples.

Example one: A parent wants to bring in cupcakes for a class because it is her daughter's birthday. Seems harmless right . . . quite sweet . . . no brainer right? *Wrong*! Here are the things that any administrator must consider:

- What if there is something in the cupcakes that makes someone sick . . . empty political cup.
- What if the answer is no: then, will it seem as a lack of acceptance of what seems to be a generous and kind offer . . . empty political cup.
- If the answer is yes then this parent and her daughter feel good . . . political cup filled.
- If the answer is yes, the students, assuming they don't get sick, will like that . . . political cup filled.
- What about the children with allergies or those who must eat gluten free? Not fair for that child . . . political cup emptied.
- If the answer is yes, the students will tell their parents what a sweet gesture that their principal allowed . . . political cup filled.
- Unless of course any parent is upset by that decision . . . political cup emptied.
- Then of course there are new laws in our state regarding food being brought in that is not in "sealed" packages and this gesture will violate that . . . political cup emptied.
- And, the cafeteria will be less than happy if they find out, as it is violating that law . . . political cup emptied.
- And, depending on how careful the students are with the cupcakes, the custodian may not be too thrilled . . . political cup emptied.
- And, if any of them complain to the superintendent that the principal did not allow the cupcakes in or that the principal did allow the cupcake in that would be bad . . . political cup emptied.
- And the teacher may not like the interruption to their instruction and they do not want to tell the student no so they need me to be the bad guy . . . political cup filled by the teacher . . . emptied by the parent.

So, the decision as the principal, based on all of these factors running was to tell the parent that they could bring in a sealed snack and have them in the conference room with their daughter during lunch. She seemed okay with that decision, but there was no question that the decision had a cost. Now there is a huge understanding that some of you are laughing right now saying, "Really? It was cupcake and it was one day. Come on!" Who is not laughing right now? Any administrator in any building who has been in this position or one like it.

They have seen it. They know it. It was not a cupcake, but a balancing act, because if anyone has been an administrator, especially a principal, they have had a cupcake dilemma before. Every decision made by any administrator is a political decision that is carefully considered and weighed before being made. Remember, there is no statement saying that every decision is made in the best interest of children. What is said is that every decision made is a political decision and that must be weighed. Let me give you a couple more examples, and allow you to decide what should be done.

1. *Do we have a pep session to celebrate the band qualifying to go to state?* (has never happened in this school before)

    - Pros—good school spirit, promoting the arts which are often overlooked, makes the band and the band directors feel appreciated, band parents feel their children are supported.
    - Cons—interruption to the learning process, shortened classes, students not in band are not impacted and probably do not care, teachers upset as this is a change from their lesson plans, parents of complaining students who had less time in class to learn what they needed to are upset with the lack of instructional time.

2. *Do we mail home transcripts at the end of the semester this year or provide them only online to save costs?*

    - Pros—cost-saving measure, parents can print as they need, saves staff time to prepare and stuff mailing, less paper usage, and parents who are computer savvy can access the information on line and saves them time.
    - Cons—parents that have no Internet access, parents that have no access to print, parents that want a hard copy, students with divorced/separated parents, upset parents as "they have always been mailed before," parents complaining that the school is too lazy to send home their own child's transcripts.

These may seem like trivial examples but any administrator, if they have ever made a decision and have heard about the other side of that decision from an upset parent or superintendent, understands the difficulty of making even "small" decisions. *Every decision comes with a political cost to any administrator and therefore sometimes causes paralysis as to making a decision at all.*

This is a common statement heard often from parents, "I swear, I just want the principal to make a decision." This statement is so ironic to any administrator because building principals, and all administrators, understand that they must weigh, debate, think through, and analyze every aspect of each decision that they make. They must consider the political fallout, evaluate their own personal political cup, consider their family and their job, then make their decision.

The solution here: allow the very people that we have hired to be in our buildings as building-level administrators run our buildings. We have to begin to trust the very people whom we have hired to be principals and superintendents to have the knowledge, the experience, and the heart to run our buildings. We have to understand that they are humans, and as long as they are being ethical, legal, and utilizing the best data- and evidence-proven strategies, they are doing the right thing and should be treated as such.

We have to remove the fear and threat of the political sands and let administrators lead and make the decisions that are in the best interests of the very children they are charged to lead. We must remove the intimidation and the sheer fear that any decision, regardless of how small or how large, can be one decision away from unemployment. No one can live that way, and we have to quit expecting our school administration to function under that stress.

Principals, too, just as their political counterparts, should devise a committee (or several depending on the school size, makeup, and interest) comprised of stakeholders to assist them and guide them in their decision making process, but we must all agree and understand that the decisions that our building-level principals and superintendents are making are decisions for the good of everyone—not just the good of the vocal few. We have to believe in our administrators and treat them with the respect they deserve and have earned if we want any continuity in our schools for our students.

Because, you see, as long as administrators know that every decision, every thought, every idea regardless of how small, may place them in the unemployment line or on the six o'clock news as the top story tonight by getting in the crosshairs of the wrong vocal parent or reporter, they will remain paralyzed and make the safe decision, not the best decision. They will run our schools with the goal of keeping the more vocal happy, regardless of the costs. Schools will not be run based on proven data or research as that may not be "popular." Schools will remain under the tyranny of the media and the vocal few that have frightened, even paralyzed, the intelligent and insightful, from making the decisions that they know are best. Schools will not move forward armed with new teaching and learning strategies that are data proven and tested, yet are "not the way we always do things" due to the fear of emptying their political cups.

This fear is paralyzing our schools and not allowing the brightest and best to move forward in assisting and educating our children. Can you imagine a doctor or scientist not being allowed to try a new therapy or treatment? Can you imagine where our lives would be without the latest and greatest technology that has now become normal to us? Can you imagine a life without all of the conveniences that were not even dreams in someone's mind years ago? We must begin to allow our schools to move forward with that same dream, with that same ingenuity, with that same drive and passion that we allow every other professional in our lives to use and to flourish. We have to! It is our children counting on it!

Curtain #6

The School Board "Experience"

In our current school system, school board members are elected to a position of service on our school boards. For the most part, with only few exceptions, they have no experience running a school and in many instances are only "serving" themselves and their own personal agendas.

The second component of the school's "leadership team" is the school board. Ah, the school board. Ask any school board member what experience they have *in running a school* and they will give you one of two responses.

1. They went to school . . . duh. They have been in school: They graduated! This includes, but is not limited to, any post-secondary degree they may or may not have had.
2. They have children in this school district. They have had children in this district. They have family/friends who have children in this school district.

So, what we are saying here is that *experience required to be on a school board (and ultimately running a school) is outlined as follows:*

Qualifying School Board Experience:

- Spending time in a school (no matter how pleasant an experience that may have been for them);
- Having children in school;
- Knowing children in school;
- Knowing someone who knows children in school;
- Having been in a school building for any period of time;
- Knowing what a school is and how it "runs" . . . for the most part;

- Knowing anyone who works at the school (past or present);
- Living in the community.

Remember, it is not valued nor measured if any of the above "experiences" are favorable toward the school system that school board members are elected to serve. If a school board member's experience with that school district is unfavorable, then that creates a whole new set of standards. School board members, for the most part, have no type of certifiable background in education. They are not, for the most part, teachers, administrators, academic coaches, nor have they had any experience *working* in schools.

They might have volunteered to work at the school, coached at the school, served on the local PTO/PTA, or been a parent volunteer for a myriad of other events at the schools, but have no *working* experience at a school; but what every school board member does have is an opinion.

As school board members read the above paragraph, they will bristle as if they are being attacked and tell you list after list of all of the things they have done, will do, have thought of doing, or are yet to do in support of the school. They will tell you story after story of the hours that they have "been at that school." They will tell you the PTO parties that they have assisted with, the money they have donated, the hours they have volunteered, the events they have attended, the games they never miss, and how much they love the school system.

Yet, the point remains that on most school boards, not one member has ever been *trained to be an educator*, let alone on how to be an instructional leader. Let's go so far as to say that they have no idea how to lead schools into the new century, where learning is diametrically different than the way that they were taught or when their children were taught and graduated.

It should make you shudder to think that if there were a poll throughout the entire United States that there would be a very small percent of school board members who went to college to become an educator, who are serving on a school districts' boards of education. There are so many things about education that shock, but this one leaves many speechless.

In the educational journey there is a clear understanding that there is sometimes a lack of experience and a need to learn and grow from others, including the school board—the very people who are leading our schools. In some instances, even over twenty years, a teacher may never see a school board member in the classroom without a building-level administrator with them. It is made clear to teachers that they are not allowed to speak to any school board member, and school board members are not allowed to come to any teacher's classroom unannounced and without the building-level administration with them.

That is simply baffling. How is the Board of Education to know what is happening in classrooms if they are not allowed to visit them? How is the

Board of Education supposed to understand what teaching is if they are not to speak to the teachers themselves? How is the school board, who is running a school, supposed to know how to run the school and the classes that they are not even visiting? How can any "governing body" such as a school board make recommendations regarding the allocation of funds in the school district when they have no idea about what a classroom teacher needs? There is a naïve assumption that all of the school board members are educated to be in the same profession—education. Not so.

This is rather embarrassing to admit that as a civilized, largely educated, nation knowing how much value we place on education, that we have the very people running our schools doing so with no correlating education. It was difficult to believe it then and I still cannot believe it now. Everyone values education, especially when it comes to our children, but this value is not reflected when we put a group of people together in some sort of popularity contest to run it? How does that, in any sense of the imagination, make sense? Why are the very people who are trained to make educational decisions being "led" by a group of people who have no experience in education?

So, how did we let this happen? How did we allow a group of people who often have no education or experience in education run our schools? And, doesn't the superintendent who *is* educated with a degree in educational administration, really run the school district anyway? Aren't school boards just there to act in an advisory capacity to make sure that the administration team fulfills its responsibility toward the school?

Don't school boards really just ensure that the superintendent does not financially bankrupt the district? Don't school boards really ensure that the school is ethically and morally right? Isn't that really the role of the Board of Education? Are they not just the *advisory board* for the superintendent? Don't they just guide, suggest, and give opinions to the superintendent who is really the person hired to run the school? Don't they just provide the superintendent the view from the shareholders who live in the district as the superintendent often does not? Is not the real role of a school board to guide, suggest, and support the superintendent with the other members of the community?

That is certainly the image that is in many minds. If you ask any random person what the role of a school board is they will tell you to guide, suggest, encourage, and support the superintendent. Well folks, if that is what you think school boards are doing, then grab a drink or a cup of coffee, because this is a secret that *all* educators know and, if they value their job, will never speak of.

School board members are elected by the public. Let's stop right here. How many of you reading this will admit that you have gone to the polls and voted for someone to be on the school board whom you do not even know?

You have no idea who they are, what they are doing in the local schools, what they stand for, or if they are a good candidate at all.

You may have seen a ton of their signs or know Ol' Bob from the shop. His wife plays euchre with your wife and you hear he is a "heck of a guy." Some would say, isn't that what all of politics are about? That may be true, but the goal of this book is to expose what is happening in *schools* so that together we can fix the problems.

We will leave politics in the larger scheme alone. We are electing well-intentioned, probably good people to run our schools, but who may, in fact, have their own agenda. We are electing nice people who, even if they don't have an agenda when they are elected, will have one if they remain on the school board for any length of time and want to be reelected. We are electing good, civic minded citizens, who may be great mechanics, great lawyers, the best dentist in town, the nicest stay at home mom, a wonderful public servant who has served in the military, and a super, local business owner, but they have no experience in running a school.

These good people, unfortunately, have no idea how a school budget works; they have no clue about the latest state standards and assessment requirements; they have no knowledge of the day-to-day running of a school building; they have never even seen the teachers teach let alone have any idea about the new evaluation system and the merit pay scale that has been put in place and how to use it. Yet, these well-intentioned, good hearted, well-meaning people are running our schools!

These school board members are good citizens with lives of their own. They do not have time to learn the standards, assess the assessments, monitor the data, evaluate teachers, assess student count and data, and keep up with the day-to-day running of any school building. Why? Because they have lives of their own. Remember, they are working their own jobs, raising their own families, and living their own lives. They hear snippets of what is happening at their schools by attending events and hearing the "talk" in the bleachers and through what information is provided to them by their superintendent, but both views are skewed at best.

Oftentimes board members get their information at a school event from a person venting about what is happening at the school and not usually venting with a collaborative, problem-solving heart. And, the school board member, depending on the person who is venting, will develop a view and form an opinion that may or may not mirror the facts; thus, with the limited information and time they have because of living their own lives, school boards are running our schools and making decisions for that school district perilously misinformed.

There is a small amount of "training" that schools are attempting to offer some school boards regarding their role in "running" the schools, but it is infrequent, insufficient, and on the time and the cost of the school board members.

Imagine if you were on the board for your local hospital and had all decision making rights . . . as our school board does when they vote. Imagine that your family member had died at that hospital, and that you felt they had not received as much care as they should have received. That would cloud your ability when votes came regarding that wing, that doctor, that nurse, and perhaps that hospital as a whole.

It does not make you vindictive or mean . . . just human. We must understand that these "agendas" are hampering the abilities of schools to move forward with decisions that educators know are best. We put the learning of countless students in the hands of these elected officials every day.

The solution to this is very easy. The school board is still a vital component of any school. The school board, however, should consist of the very stakeholders who live and work in the school district. They are the taxpayers and are the most affected by the financial decisions made by a school. Is electing them the best way to get the "right people" on our school boards? This proposition would be a balance of both.

Allowing the democratic voices of citizens to be heard is important, after all this is America, but if we insist on voting school board members to our schools, then we must include other stakeholders who would love to serve their schools but may never be elected, or even want to run. We should and could have several school board (committees) with varying levels of expertise in each of those "boards" to assist and serve their part of the school.

For example, wouldn't a local mechanic be a great member to assist his local school in the bus garage? Doesn't it make sense that a data programmer who lives in the community would be a wonderful asset in looking at the data of our schools and assisting us in providing teachers a meaningful way to use those data? Wouldn't it be wonderful if the local attorney living in our community read all of the documents prepared by the school board to ensure that they are legal and will propel the school in the direction that we want to go based on the new federal guidelines?

And, how about the local construction worker or man that owns his own engineering firm? Wouldn't he be a great asset for the leaking roof on the elementary school? Or, how about the CPA? He could ensure that we are using our funds appropriately and getting the most bang for our buck. Doesn't that just make sense?

Without question the solution here is to have a larger school board comprised of both elected and named stakeholders from both the community and the school. Together this "board" or "boards" could make a huge difference in moving our schools forward into the next century. The more "expertise" that we can bring to our schools the better. Finally, the school board must also consist and must include the very teachers and administrators that the decisions are being made to impact. These educators must be involved in the decision making process of the school board. Why are we not doing that? Again just common sense.

Curtain #7

The "Power" of the School Board

Before going any further let's make sure that this point is very clear regarding just what kind of "power" the school board actually has in school systems. This "power" will help you understand why no educator will broach the topic of any school board member to anyone who they think could or would repeat it.

We may live in a democratic society, and everything said about school board members in that "governing body" is vital, but, make no mistake, no educator will get on the wrong side of a school board member and remain in that school system long enough to talk about it. Every teacher learns very quickly the power of the school board and how vital it is to "stay under their radar."

The way it is supposed to work, the school board has the ability to hire and fire the superintendent. The superintendent has the ability to hire and fire any of the administration/leadership team. The leadership team/administration has the ability to hire and fire any staff/teachers working in their building, but it all trickles back to the school board. Here are a couple of examples witnessed first-hand. Remember, almost every teacher knows this and will not tell you this—unless they trust you and know it will not get back to the school board.

STORY #1

Teacher A had a student in her class to whom she gave detention for talking in class. The student went home and told his father who just happened to be on the school board. The school board member and father called the superintendent questioning the detention. The superintendent encouraged the school board member to speak to the teacher as a parent—not as a school board member.

The school board member did indeed call the teacher, but even after the teacher explained her perspective on what happened in class that day which warranted the detention, the school board member did not agree with the detention. The teacher stated that the detention would stand (bold move on the teacher's part), and the school board member expressed displeasure in that decision. The school board member called the superintendent back expressing his concern and the superintendent called the principal.

The principal called the teacher to his office to gain a greater understanding of the situation that caused the detention. After hearing the teacher's story, he supported the teacher. The principal called the superintendent and explained the classroom situation and why he did indeed support the teacher. The superintendent tried to reason with the board member in support of the principal.

Good, right? All resolved, right? Teacher feels supported, student is disciplined, superintendent supported the teacher, and principal feels supported. All is good right? Wrong. After the detention had been served, the school board member continued to pick and pick at every decision that the teacher made and gained the support of other board members until the superintendent could no longer politically support the teacher or the principal. Future decisions made by that teacher were often not supported and frequently overturned—until the teacher, the principal, the superintendent, or all three leave.

STORY #2

Recently, a newly elected school board member has a talented son who had been very involved in choir and theater ever since elementary school. A new choir director has been hired after the old, well-loved, choir director retired. The school board member is not overly pleased with the new director and has made many comments throughout the school year to many other parents regarding the lack of time and attention her son is getting as compared to the old choir director.

Other school board members are getting on board and having some "off the record" conversations between the superintendent and the school board member, between the principal and the superintendent, and between the principal and the teacher. Nonetheless, as the spring musical approaches, the son does not get the role he wanted (mind you he got a bigger role, but not the role he wanted), and there was so much pressure that the choir director changed the role to the one the student wanted to "smooth" things over. Finding a win-win solution was what the teacher was told to do.

STORY #3

Two students were academically neck and neck heading into their senior year. They had almost identical GPAs since their freshman year. They had taken virtually mirrored courses, both weighted and non-weighted throughout all of high school. Over the summer, before their senior year, one of the students took what they believed to be a weighted class to "win" and become valedictorian of the senior class. The school maintained that since the class was not offered at the school it could not be counted as weighted if taken over the summer; therefore, since their GPA's were tied, there would be co-valedictorians that year.

The parents would hear nothing of that decision as their child had taken the class over the summer with, what they stated, were the "blessings of the school" (though no one had ever agreed to that) and had "beat" the other student fair and square and should not be "co-" valedictorian but rather valedictorian. There was meeting after meeting with the parents, the school board, principals, and counselors and on and on and on. The decision stood; they would be co-valedictorians. Graduation came and went and everyone moved on, right? Wrong. The end result: the principal and the superintendent "left" within a few years after the parent had two of their friends elected to serve on the school board.

Again, there are countless stories just like these. The scenarios are all the same. School boards have a tremendous amount of political pull in the communities. They are making decisions based on information from a few select parents who speak the loudest, go to the media, threaten to go to the media, or use bullying tactics to get their way. They are elected officials who, if they want to be re-elected, will do as their constituents want. We all know what is happening in our government with elected officials, so how can we think our schools are safe from that bureaucracy and political maneuvering?

What is being said here very clearly is that the very same political bureaucracy and political maneuvering that is happening in Washington, DC, is happening right here in our schools. The problem is that students and their futures are being manipulated for the benefit and personal agenda of adults. There will probably be other things in this book that rile some people up, but nothing will rile people as much as these few pages will. If you think, as only time as a teacher and as an administrator can reveal, that school board members are members of the community who guide, support, and encourage the superintendent, you are living in a fantasy world and every educator knows it.

Everyone wants the best for your child. No parent would ever question any other parent who pushes their child, who wants the best for them, and who watches and protects them. After all, isn't that just good parenting?

The difference that is being made here is that when you are an *elected official* on a school board, your focus is expected to be the good of *all* students in that school, not your own political agenda, your own children, the children of your friends, your children's friends or teammates, but every child in that school. Yet, for too many school boards, that is not the case and good, educated, amazing instructional leaders are being run out on a rail, because they got on the wrong side of a school board member or two.

Those in education witness the power of school board members whose children were swimmers, athletes, singers, or valedictorians. Every decision that that school board member made was through the lens of making programs better in the best interest of their child. Far too often the "favor" of the school board member becomes the "project" of the superintendent and, ultimately, the principal. Any idea that does not sit well or might be in contradiction to what the school board wants will be killed or thwarted until that school board member is gone.

Once, while speaking to an attorney as a building-level principal, I found myself caught in the cross hairs of a school board member. If you Google my name, you will see how I was represented in the media and in conflict with the school board. Shall we pause here while you use Google?

Welcome back. That statement is made in giving full disclosure. My own experiences have assisted me throughout this entire book to make many of my points. There is nothing to hide! There was no mistake on my part! The decisions made were ones that could still be lived with! Every decision, as a building-level principal that, based on all of the facts, not just those reported or shared, were made in the best interest of the building and all of the students in it at the time.

Through first-hand experience, my understanding of what it means to be on the "wrong" side of a school board and what that can, and did, do for employment in my school district is a reality felt personally. I am not trying to vent or present myself as a victim. I am trying to make very clear that going against what a school board member wants will have major consequences for that administrator.

Choose to stand up to a school board member and you are immediately one day closer to your last day in that school system, regardless of students' needs. Put something before the agenda of a school board's agenda and you are, as a building-level principal, one day closer to leaving that school district. To push away from the agenda made from your school board both subtly and more overtly, and you will find yourself in a contract that will "not be renewed" because you are "just not a good fit for the school district."

Anyway, the attorney said, "There are two different types of principals: those that have been fired by a school board and those that are yet to be fired by a school board." After hanging up the phone, I felt a huge sadness. Not sadness for myself and my situation, but sadness that this is what the educational system envisioned by her as a young teacher for so many years ago as that child at the kitchen table playing school was becoming.

Since then, watching countless administrative colleagues go by the wayside because of a school board member only deepens that sadness. Watching and seeing amazing administrators not fire ineffective teachers because that teacher was on the good side of a school board member; watching in disbelief as highly effective principals who have led their school to amazing letter grades, great test scores, and amazing accolades were "let go" due to an upset school board member with their own agenda; watching great teachers leave a school district due to a school board member; each and every time seeing this and wondering what had happened.

How can we as an intelligent, forthright, forward thinking people allow this to happen to our students? Why are we not doing what every administrator knows is right? How can the agenda of an elected official called a school board member have such political power? How did we as a society let that happen? Then the answer hit me. The public does not know!

The public, or most parents who are not "in" education, send their children off to school for an education. They know their teachers and may or may not know their administrators. They may or may not have even voted for the school board members and certainly do not attend school board meetings (unless there is something directly impacting them or their child), so they have no idea what decisions are being made which directly affect their child. They, if they knew better, would not stand for it, so hopefully this voice will open this curtain.

The solution for this issue is really easy. There is complete support for electing members of the community to serve on school boards, but their power must be balanced. We must allow our schools to be run by the *educated administrators* who have the knowledge and experience to do so. We must return our school board members to advising, supporting, and encouraging our administration and remove any school board member who has an agenda which is not in line with that vision. We must have the difficult conversations with outspoken, out-of-place, misguided, agenda-filled and personal views of too many school board members.

This is an easy fix, and, for some very lucky schools, not a problem. There also must be a clarification that there are some school boards that are functioning in this capacity, but they are one decision, one election, one school board member from going the other way. We must restore our schools to the experienced, educated administrators who seek guidance and input and lead their buildings.

Unfortunately until we do that, we will have buildings run by inexperienced administrators who are looking for a paycheck not the calling to serve our children. No one will stay for the amount of time required to truly change the tides necessary for education if they know they are one decision away from upsetting the school board and losing their jobs. No one can live that way, and no one should have to, especially when our children are at stake.

Curtain #8

What is Really Happening in Our Schools Today?

If you looked inside classrooms today, unfortunately, they are not very different from those one room schoolhouses of yesteryear. As a matter of fact, classrooms today, in many schools, do not reflect research and development's latest definition of what "good" teaching is.

There is one thing that is certain, you do not need to search long for an opinion about what should be taught, who should teach it, when it should be taught, for how long it should be taught, why it should be taught, or if it should be even taught at all. The opinions are sometimes deafening. These opinions are found throughout the media; there are special news correspondents investigating schools; there are politicians venting and ranting and there are parents, students, and teachers at odds over that same definition of what "good" is.

The argument is so deep and so divided that there seems to be no end in sight. Some may even have forgotten what the argument is anymore. What is happening in classrooms today has become such a politically charged question that it is leaving the very people in the center of it, the educators, lost.

- There have been studies against lecturing, and then studies proving that due to the lack of lecturing our students do not know the necessary information.
- There are books, professional development, and movements suggesting that students should have technology in their hands and learn only through technology; then there are contradicting studies suggesting that students should "disconnect" from technology as they are not engaged, but instead hooked to their technology.

- There are studies that say students must be entertained and engaged in their learning and contrary studies that say that students are too overly stimulated and should not be so engaged and entertained.
- There are readings to suggest that students should learn at their own pace and not be placed in grades or in subjects or even receive letter grades but rather demonstrate their learning and move at their own pace, yet colleges and the post-secondary world and even employers clearly cannot and are not ready for the ten-year-old who has learned at his or her own pace and is ready to enter college or, even better the work force.
- There are countless stories that suggest that schools need to do away with seat time. Seat time is defined by the amount of time that students must be in the seat of a classroom before they can receive credit for the class. Many states have abandoned laws stating that if a child can take a test and prove mastery they do not need to attend the class at all and may receive credit for the class. Then the other side of the argument states that students' attendance is awful at schools and it is now trickling down to the workforce as they enter careers, so schools should make them come to school.
- There are those who believe that traditional public schools are not doing what is right by their students, so a myriad of charter and private schools have arisen, yet there are those that will compare the data and make claims that the data of success for those schools is not so compelling to win the argument that they are "better."
- There is argument after argument over the new standards and what our students should be learning and what is still "core" curriculum and those that would argue that "what we learned before" is just fine.
- There are those who believe that we need to return to the three R's of reading, 'riting and 'rithmetic, but others think we need to teach more globally and open our students to more possibilities.
- There are those who believe that morals and values must be taught in our schools and others that become very angry at the idea that anyone other than the parents should be or would be teaching their children right from wrong.
- There are those who believe that sports should play an important role in schools and monies should be placed to that end, and others who believe that sports have little value and therefore monies should be placed elsewhere.
- There is study after study showing that students engaged in a fine art such as music or theater are more successful in school, and therefore, those programs should be enriched. The other side does not believe that and does not see value for the arts for our schools and is cutting the programs.

- There have been movements pushing for smaller class sizes for the success of students and other studies that have shown that class size did little to differentiate student achievement.
- There have been movements to "track" students based on their abilities and studies that have shown that there is no value in doing such.
- There have been suggestions to do away with a letter grade, period, and only track student mastery, but this movement has fallen on deaf ears as a student transfers to a post-secondary or another school district that relies on the letter grade for student placement and rank.
- There have been movements to eliminate the valedictorian and salutatorian of the class stating that they have little or no value to post-secondary success, and parents of those students (either past, present, or future) who would have your heads roll at such a stupid idea.
- There are teachers who believe lecturing is the way to go, others who do not, and there are equally as many arguments to support either side.
- There are those who argue that parental involvement is the key to a student's success and those who, depending on the parent or the socioeconomic abilities of the parent, believe that parent involvement is more of a hindrance than a help.
- There are some who believe that cursive should still be taught in schools, while others believe that cursive is outdated and serves no purpose.
- There are those who believe that the way to measure students' success is to test them with one test or another; then, there are others who don't even know what we are testing anymore and don't believe that a child's success can be defined by one test.

Again, this could go on and on for pages upon pages, but here is the point: What is happening in our classrooms today is sheer and utter confusion. All of the political jockeying between politicians, educators, and parents causes confusion that gets passed on to the classroom.

Each and every politician nowadays has a stance on education. You see those opinions passed to the state government, who pass them to the state superintendent of instruction, who pass them on to superintendents, who pass them on to principals, who pass them on to teachers, who pass them on to their students.

Have you have ever played the telephone game? The telephone game is a game often played to demonstrate how each of us hears things differently and that much can get lost in translation. One person, in a line of people, whispers something to the person next to him. The something that was whispered continues to be whispered to the person next in line until the last person says aloud what he heard.

Laughter usually erupts because, depending on how many people there are, nothing comes out like what was said in the first place. The point:

Educational politicians are playing the telephone game; and the best of intentions and possibly the implementation of best practices are virtually unrecognizable by the time they reach the classroom.

This constant "loss in translation" is leading to mass confusion, and superintendents are left to "interpret" what they hear at the other end of the telephone line. Sometimes that interpretation is accurate and at other times, it is not. There have been countless examples for many of us in education where decisions were made regarding what was being taught that were based on information provided in July before school started only to find out in October that that information was either inaccurate, misread, or headed in the opposite direction we were going in and had to change course immediately.

That frustration is large for a building-level principal, as a difference exists between the "interpretations" of what has been passed down by law and how that implementation plays out in classrooms. There is no question that one principal's interpretation is different from another's, and therein lies the constant confusion.

When the teacher, principal, or the superintendent changes course midstream, to parents it often looks like a lack of clarity, order, or leadership in their child's school when that is not at all the case. What makes things even more confusing is that this "focus" can change from one school district to another, let alone from one state to another.

There have been several opportunities for me to witness and be a part of conversations with groups of highly educated teachers who couldn't reach consensus. What one believes to be true regarding a standard, or a test, or a requirement may be diametrically different than what another teacher believes to be true and is doing in their classroom—and this is a group of educated people all "in" education and all having attended a meeting or having read the newest law or mandate. Even we cannot agree. No wonder there is confusion.

There are far too many times as meetings were happening with groups of intelligent, college-educated principals that arguments erupted regarding the interpretation and follow-through required regarding state or governmental mandates. Sitting back and watching principals and other administrators argue their interpretation of a mandate to the death, would leave one wondering and confused about the entire process, let alone the mandate or agenda being discussed.

If the very people who are carrying out mandates are this divided and confused, can you even imagine what is going to happen when it reaches our schools?

So, why is this happening? Remember, education has become a political platform. What is "right" and "good" in our classrooms today has, more so than ever before, become open to debate and subject to public opinion. Just let that rest with you a moment. What your child is learning, will learn, or needs to learn is being debated and decided on not by the educator in front of your child but rather by some political platform. What the outcome will be depends on who "wins."

All of this leaves teachers confused and frustrated since they are always aiming at a moving target and, depending on the year, they might not even have the right ammunition to fire at the target. There will be a discussion about teachers in a later chapter, but if the very person who is delivering the content is not sure of its clarity, how can we expect results? In any given year, a teacher can be sure that the following may change based on the needs, wants, or political movements made in that year.

1. What will the assessment for the course be? (This is especially true for courses that are state tested.)
2. When will they know what is on the assessment?
3. Will they be giving all parts of the assessment or just a section of it?
4. Will they be teaching to the test for the entire year?
5. What materials will be needed or will they have?
6. When will the test be given, and when will the results be returned?
7. How will they be held accountable for the results?
8. How will the class impact other courses like it?
9. What happens when they change the assessment two weeks before it even starts?
10. How can cohort data be compared when they change the test every year?

There are those of you reading this, who are not educators and are saying, "Please! Are you kidding me?" Teachers and administrators know this happens every year, and every one of them is laughing that you are even asking that question because the answer is *no*. The confusion starts at the top and trickles back down within our own walls of education.

College educators want to prepare their students for the workforce and are looking for high schools to send graduates prepared to learn at a post-secondary level. High schools are looking for middle schools to prepare their students, not only for state testing but to learn at the rigor level necessary and with the appropriate content to graduate them ready for the post-secondary or employment world.

Middle schools are looking toward elementary schools to send students to them who are reading on grade level, prepared in the necessary math skills, and ready to tackle the middle school social issues so that they can prepare them for high school. Elementary schools are looking toward pre-K programs (if the students have access to them) to teach what used to equate to kindergarten learning before they even come to school so that they can provide the necessary skills before sending their students off to middle school.

And pre-K programs are looking for parents to send their four- to five-year-old off to school with the social and educational knowledge necessary for them to be successful in elementary school. Overwhelming when you think about it, isn't it? So, where does that leave students who do not have the skills, support, or knowledge to be prepared for the level they are entering in school? You guessed it! Behind.

So, what is happening in our schools today? Confusion, a lack of clarity, and a lack of focus. Due to the political maneuvering and social pressures, educators and administrators are left to find their own way through this educational maze. We do so, just as in a real maze, by hitting dead ends, turning around and doing it again, fixing our mistakes, and hoping we get out on time with the right tools. That does not seem like the best way to run the educational system that we, as a society, rely upon.

There seems that there must be a better way of all pulling together in the same direction toward the same goal, doesn't there? It seems so logical to me that it seems impossible that it even needs to be said. What is happening in the classrooms will improve for our students when we all answer these very simple questions.

1. What do we want our students to know?
2. At what level or grade?
3. How will we all measure it?
4. What will we define as mastery of that knowledge?
5. How will we put interventions into place for those who have not mastered it and what will that look like?

What was just written is not rocket science folks. It is common sense, yet it is *lost* on today's policymakers and in today's classrooms. What you have today is a group of well-intentioned teachers and administrators who are walking around like balls in a pinball machine being bounced from one "directive" to another. So, the first step is to clear up the confusion and provide clear, meaningful direction.

Curtain #9

Teachers and Their "Training"

Okay, so this is the chapter that every educator may have fanned to first after looking at the table of contents. This is the chapter that every teacher is ready for. They have heard it before, they watch it on TV, and they read it in every news story; they are ready for what they are accustomed to—an attack. They are ready for this chapter and are ready to pounce on the words that may be coming next. They are ready to defend, to explain, to argue, and to appease.

But, there is another group of teachers who are reading this chapter ready for yet another attack from a long list of attacks made on our profession. They may not be willing to pounce, because they are, frankly, too exhausted to pounce. They have succumbed to the "let them say whatever they are going to say" attitude and are, frankly, tired. Well, teachers, rest easy. This is neither an attack nor a hall pass (love the analogy there, huh), it is a statement of what has been observed, with which you will in all likelihood agree.

It is not intended to damn, but to expose. It is neither a grenade nor a white flag. It is what we all know is true if we really search ourselves and ask ourselves questions. Remember, I spent thirty-plus years in education and I am right there beside you. This comes from a proud teacher who taught high school students. This is from someone who has walked your walk for many, many years. Mine is the perspective of an assistant principal, who assisted teachers with the discipline and attendance of their students and who finally served as a principal. This vantage point and experience has seen all sides. With that being said, know your voice.

> First let me begin with the fact that when it comes to training teachers to teach, we have an old outdated system throughout most of the United States. The fact is that colleges are still preparing teachers in many of the same ways as they did thirty-plus years ago.

Rest on that statement for just a moment. Teachers graduating today are being prepared to teach the students of today with the preparation of yesterday. Does that strike anyone else as just plain ludicrous?

Tons of educational colleges and universities just puckered and are offended. They are ready to provide you a curriculum as proof that this statement is just plain false and that this constitutes a lack of understanding of their programs. With the space and distance of thirty years from graduation, colleges and universities could question this reference to current graduation requirements.

Those same universities would question one's ability to understand their most recent pedagogical changes and in righteous indignation question the ability to even make such comment. So then, how could it validly be made? How could that be known? How could that be an experience, given the time of separation from my own college experience?

This is based on solid experience—time in the field. This view has been developed as an administrator who has been hiring teachers for the past ten years, as well as working with countless other administrators throughout other school districts and other states who are all saying the same things. So, if you are from higher education and you are reading or you wonder how our teachers are not graduating from college prepared with the necessary tools to do their jobs, then take this opportunity to look at these words as knowledge—not an attack.

Look at them as your opportunity to enhance the preparation of our teachers, rather than an attack on your school and what it may or may not be doing. View them as your contribution to resolving the problems, and pioneer the change in preparation that our teachers need. And we all know: When you know better, you do better. So, to educational post-secondary teacher preparation colleges and universities, here is what every administrator who has ever hired a new teacher and what every first year teacher knows, but will not often tell you.

In the preparation of teachers there has been very little change from the pedagogy of the past to the pedagogy of today, which provides teachers with insufficient tools. Most of the problem is that the majority of a teacher's preparation time is spent in a classroom learning the pedagogy and philosophy of how to teach, and minimal time is spent in the classroom learning about methodology of teaching or gaining the necessary "tools" for their teaching toolbox.

Additionally, there is also little to no additional training or resources once they have graduated. As a principal, there have been multiple opportunities in which countless teachers were hired from several universities both in-state and out of it and the frustration is unexplainable. It does not seem to matter the training or college or university they graduated from, teachers fresh out of college come to the table with this: a mouthful of pedagogy and no substance to back it up.

Sure, they have a lovely portfolio: they have spent hours preparing for their methods class, but that portfolio is useless in a real classroom. They know how to *say* how to "engage" students with the right answers, yet have no idea how to do that in their classroom on Tuesday. They know how to *say* the correct answer as to how to deal with an unruly parent or student, but are frustrated when it happens and the response they were "taught" blows up in their face.

Every time a new teacher was hired and they "hit the wall" for the first time, the heart breaks for them. Building-level principals, who just hired them, recognize that there was a harsh reality coming in stark contrast with what they have been sold regarding the "idea" of what it is to be a teacher through their university and the reality of what our profession is. The reality begins when:

- The pedagogy of teaching and training taught in university or college must be relearned in light of what teaching is in reality, when thirty ninth-graders are staring you down waiting for your next move.
- You need a new way to understand that the parent you spoke to last night, upset about their child's grade on the test, does not at all care about what your university told you about testing, testing questions, and testing research that you shared with her last night. They want to know how to fix it or why the question was marked wrong.
- An explanation will have to be given to you to assist you in understanding that, as a new teacher, you will have to justify everything you do in class from the homework assignment you give to the lesson taught to the assessment you used to measure learning. And, no, some parents and students will still think that, despite your best explanation of the lesson, the homework, or the test, that you are stupid and are just out to "get their child."
- An administrator will have to give you the painful explanation that the parent call you received the previous night was not an attack on you, but a request to clarify questions.
- You will need to be educated and cautioned in regards to the teacher's workroom and why frequenting the workroom and who is in the workroom may or may not be a good fit for you to go there.
- You will need to be talked off of the ledge the first time a student tells you to go you know where, because you could not understand why they were not in love with Shakespeare.
- It will have to be explained to you that while you love "insert whatever topic here," not every student will, and your job is to teach them how to, at least, appreciate it.

- It will have to be sold to you that it is worth it when you have spent nine hours grading papers that no one seemed to do right and you just do not know why.
- You will have to be sold the idea that it will get better.
- You will have to be consoled as the explanation is made that despite what those parents just called you and the names that they used against you, that you can still forge a relationship with them. Try to not take it personally.
- You will have to be assured that though teaching seems tough, and seems like it will never get better, it will; or, at least, experience suggests it will.
- You will be encouraged that each year will get easier, when you have spent another weekend grading papers and making lesson plans, only to realize that they were thrown out by Tuesday.
- Your administrator will have to give you a salesman-like pitch to make you believe that despite the less than stellar evaluation you just received (after all you were a straight A student in college), you are a good teacher and you are going to get better in time with more practice.
- You will need to be reminded that, even though you are the teacher, you sometimes make mistakes and you will have to apologize for them. That we, as teachers, are not perfect and we have to, sometimes, change our mind, go back on our word, change the plans, admit our mistakes, and offer no other words than sorry.
- There will need to be a full-on sales force effect to convince you that despite the amount of money on your paycheck, which certainly does not match your education, you are getting rewards far greater than money (and hope your mortgage company feels the same way).
- There will be an offering of "summers off" while your other friends in college are making far more money than you.
- Others will insist that despite the proportion of your paycheck that is now going back to pay off your university or college, it will get better in time. However, depending on the school, the amount of debt, and the pay, that may not be really true.
- Then, a take back will happen when you spend most of your breaks and summers attending workshops, doing lesson plans, and preparing for the upcoming week/semester/year. Hopefully you won't catch on to that one yet.
- And, finally, for the good teachers, the ones who are and who will make a difference, there will be full-out begging and whatever it takes to try to convince you to stay in this field, to stick it out because our children are counting on you.

These are the issues administrators deal with every day in their offices. Sometimes for parents, sometimes for students, but most often for teachers, the tissues were kept at the ready, as experience and love talked them through their tears.

Through their time at their college or university there had not been substantial exposure to any real classroom situation to show what it really meant to be a teacher on a day-to-day basis. Despite what they had heard from their college or university, nothing hurts as much as realizing, after you have graduated from college with a degree in teaching, that this indeed may not be the career for you.

As their "boss," I witnessed the utter disappointment in new teachers' eyes the moment when they realized that they have just spent the past four years (and a ton of money) to know that they are not prepared for tomorrow, let alone getting through the remainder of the semester. There was an exorbitant amount of time needed to get new teachers to where they really needed to be to be good educators, and, as an administrator, I also knew that more time was needed than existed in the day. As a human being, I felt sickness and sorrow.

That realization came while looking in the eyes of a fellow educator and realizing that this may break them and that we, as a society, will lose another great educator due to their lack of training and resources. Knowing that as these young, new teachers come to the realization that the income they are making will barely cover the cost of their student loans, let alone the cost of living, administrators listen. Sometimes, all that can be done is to comfort, cry a lot inside, and know deep down that this could have all been avoided with proper training.

Early on in some teachers' careers there are many opportunities to learn some of the same lessons listed above—not from college but on the job.

There are those who are now thinking, "Well, isn't that true of any profession? Really, Cathy, every career gets better with years of experience, right? Do you think teaching should be any different?" The response is, "Yes! Oh, my God, yes." We are not just any field where mistakes can be afforded while waiting for a teacher to get better. Perhaps this question will quell those who think that we just need to allow teachers to be ill-trained and get better with time. Whose child are we willing to sacrifice in the ill-equipped teacher's classroom? Yours? Are you still asking the same question? Probably not!

You are right that many, well any, professional gets better at their trade the more and more that they do it. That is an obvious statement. The issue in education is this: Your child's teacher is "getting better" at the cost of a child, or in reality, at the cost of a room full of children. In only a few universities is there significant exposure to the classroom early on, much earlier than many of the teachers hired by this administrator.

But that time in the classroom was in the role of an observer. There was a "looking" at the classroom, giving opinions about the classroom, but there was no getting the hands dirty, so to speak. There is never any communication with a parent until student teaching begins. There is never an opportunity afforded to even speak to a principal or any other administrator until being hired and starting teaching. There was never an opportunity to have received any form of "evaluation" other than the opinion of college professors, which is nothing like what a formal teacher evaluation looks like. There was no exposure to the work load that is expected for a teacher.

There is a small indication given on lesson planning from the college (which was nothing like the real thing when teaching began), but there had never been any exposure to a curriculum map, to state standards, or to how the knowledge was to align with assessments. There was never an opportunity provided to speak with the other teachers, to learn from them, hear their experiences, gain materials from them, look for resources from them, and just get help.

The teaching career has teachers graduating and teaching immediately the next fall. In the classroom next door there may be an experienced teacher who allows the new teacher to question, to learn from, and to borrow materials—a true colleague, a mentor, and a friend. Even as Facebook friends, there will never be enough space or time to offer the amount of thanks these teachers deserve. There is a comfort level with them that encourages novices to ask not only how to teach something, but possibly even teach it for them and allow them to watch.

These teachers are a resource. Under their guidance young teachers became stronger, more confident, and far more capable, but they do this out of the kindness of their hearts. What about those new teachers being placed in a smaller school where they are the only one teaching their subject? Or, what would those new teachers do who do not have such a relationship with their colleagues? Or, what about the new teachers hired when both teachers teaching that subject are new? Then what? Remember, teachers are graduating from college with a cute portfolio and a ton of pedagogy and opinions but *no real tools*.

Can you imagine a mechanic walking into the garage for his first day of work, a car pulls in to have work done, and he is not provided with a single tool? Would you let him work on your car? Or imagine a surgeon preparing to remove your appendix with nothing, not a single tool, nurse, or proper materials in order for your surgery to be a success. Would you be that patient? If you have ever hired an attorney to represent you, one would assume you would know that they have had the exposure and resources to gain the case knowledge necessary to defend you.

Are you okay with them telling you, "I have never done any cases before, but I will hope for the best"? No, even attorneys know having co-council on new attorneys' cases is imperative. And remember, the "tools" necessary for teaching, for the most part, cannot be purchased. You cannot go to Walmart or even a teacher supply store and get that great engaging activity to use in your fourth period reading class tomorrow. There is no section in the mall where you can go purchase that great assessment for your algebra class to measure how your students have learned. Remember, until you started your first teaching job, you may not have even known what you were teaching and for sure had no resources to teach it.

It is without question that there are some of you reading this that are saying, "Come on Cathy, you cannot compare a surgeon or an attorney to a teacher!" Really? Who do you think is the person who taught your surgeon to operate on you? Let me pause here while you remove your foot from your mouth. That is right, a teacher. And, who taught your dentist to remove your aching tooth? Again, you are right, a teacher. And, who is the person that is caring for your family member right now? That lovely nurse? Yup, taught by a teacher. And who is that person who taught your attorney the law? Again, you guessed it, a teacher.

This idea could keep going and going but this is the point to be made here: No one questions that our system is broken, but, the reality comes down to this . . . are you, as a parent, willing to allow your son or daughter to be in the classroom of a teacher who is prepared with pedagogy, but with no tools or real knowledge to do the task? Remember your child will have one shot to be in kindergarten, one shot to take that AP class they need for their scholarship, and one shot to be in that algebra class that they need to master in order to pass the state test. Are you willing to risk that?

Please make no mistake, this is not an attack on first-year teachers. We were all there! Everyone has to start somewhere and that is *not* the point being made here. My new teachers have heard me say, and though it is shameful to say it out loud, "My first year of teaching, my students learned in spite of me not because of me."

The point that is being made is to highlight the lack of support, guidance, and professional development provided to first-year teachers. As any first-year teacher does, we muddled through doing the best we knew how, but we know we were not prepared, and we did not teach the best. The first years are not an example in which there was adequate or effective preparation compared to that of an experienced teacher teaching a classroom of students.

This is all being said to understand that the beginnings of "fixing" our system start with the education and preparation of our teachers. Until we look at what is best for our teachers and ultimately our students and not what is in the best interest of the pocketbooks of our colleges and universities, then we are destined to continue to be where we are. Until we, as a society, scream from the rooftops and demand that our teachers have the proper preparation and walk into their first year prepared, armed with materials and some experience to deal with what is coming for them, then new teachers will continue to "learn" how to teach, get armed, and gain the materials they need to teach on the backs of our children.

When you think about it, no other field graduates their students from college (or specific training) and sends them off to the rest of their career to "do their job." Remember, this is not a professional who may turn the wrong pipe down, or someone who may have missed a meeting; these are people who are educating our children. Every study will tell you that if a child is not learning and is not educated appropriately, based on their specific grade level or class, they will be behind for the rest of their lives. The stakes are so high for teachers, yet we send teachers into classrooms to teach with a semester (or less) of student teaching and whatever support the school district has in place to support them.

Colleges are preparing teachers with the content (subject matter) necessary and the pedagogy, but not the hands-on, day-to-day teaching that may have driven potentially weak teachers from the profession in the first place. Remember, by the time students are in student teaching, they are in the last semester of their senior year. This is awfully late to realize that perhaps education was not the right field for them.

This is a really easy fix: by getting potential educational candidates away from the educational pedagogy of the university and into the classrooms as often and as soon as possible. It is there, in the very schools that they hope to work one day, that they will learn far more than being told about what a classroom will be like. Put them there to feel, see, and hear what the classroom will be like. We must also work, as schools, with the post-secondary colleges and universities by assisting each other in understanding what tools a teacher must have when they graduate in order to come to school ready to teach armed with tools in their tool box.

The fix lies in the training. There must be a better balance of pedagogy and methodology. We have to balance "learning" about how to teach with "teaching." Students who are interested in a career in education should be in classrooms in real buildings from day one. They must be in the very classrooms they hope to lead one day. They should spend a balanced amount of time in the first couple of years learning how to teach and mirroring that by working with actual teachers who are teaching. They can begin by teaching "mini lessons" several times a month. They can and should then move on to more time in the schools than at their universities by their last two years.

Student teaching should be no less than an entire semester. Most educators, especially administrators, would suggest an entire year. Teaching kindergarten students in August is much different than teaching seniors in May. Prospective teachers should be exposed to as many different teachers, teaching styles, subjects, and disciplines as they will be licensed to teach. There is no excuse for allowing students to graduate from a university or college with no experience in the classroom that they want to teach. Graduates (future educators), depending on the discipline or subject they are teaching, will struggle to find a job and will struggle worse with students once they have one.

Once the new teacher enters the school system and is hired, they must be provided additional assistance, at a minimum, on a weekly basis. This should be part of the expectation of the university or college and should be paid for by that university or college.

Schools must work in partnership with colleges and universities to assist them in understanding where the strengths and shortcomings are in their teacher preparation classes from the very practitioners in the field. Through that partnership and collaboration, the college or university can prepare teachers to enter the classroom not only armed with the pedagogy necessary, but the materials and ongoing support to be successful.

Finally, colleges and universities should work hand-in-hand with school administrators to ensure that the prospective teacher understands other vital aspects of teaching from an administrative standpoint. These include:

- Teacher evaluation system
- Observations versus evaluation
- Lesson planning expectations
- Classroom management
- Teaching strategies and expectations
- Professional development
- Grading rubrics
- Grading practices and scales
- Day to day practices
- Supervision versus facilitation in the classrooms
- Learning from others

This is such an easy fix that it leaves one scratching their head as to why we are not doing it. Clearly, it is true that we all value our teachers, and we expect that they are trained appropriately to teach. Yet, every educator will tell you that that is not happening and with some very small modifications we can change that, so when will we?

Curtain #10

Professional Development for Our Teachers

After a teacher graduates and enters his or her classroom, the professional development of that teacher falls on both the teacher and the school system in which they teach. There are, unfortunately, not many additional professional development opportunities for teachers. There are some school districts that provide opportunities for professional development one day here, one day there, but most schools do not have the time in their required school day nor the resources to really keep teachers current on the newest pedagogy or training.

Remember, for most school districts to provide professional development, they must remove the teacher from the very classroom where they are needed the most. Schools are not like most companies who can remove their employees from their offices or their desks for a day(s) and tell their clients that they are away from their desks or out of the office to provide them the necessary training in order to keep them tuned and skilled at their trade.

Most schools do not have the opportunity to do as any other professional organization does and offer training during the work day. If teachers are to be trained "during their work day," it leaves a classroom(s) not learning due to the absence of their teacher. Many schools used to provide time *during* their school year by building in professional development days for teachers, but due to outcries from parents, families, and budget cuts, those days have all but gone by the wayside.

Some schools have created modified schedules shortening a school day once a week or a few times a month. But, again, due to the outcries of families and the need for daycare if the schools release early, many schools are feeling the pressure to abandon any time during the school day or school year for professional development opportunities.

So, what that leaves us is the fact that most teachers are left having to leave the classroom for a day or more to gain the professional development which quite often comes at their own personal cost. Some schools are better at allocating resources and time and will allow teachers to attend local conferences for their disciplines at the schools' expense. That, unfortunately, is becoming a rarity rather than a norm. Many schools, due to the continual budget cuts and pressures of the school day and year, have all but eliminated professional development opportunities for their teachers.

When my teaching career began the district did an amazing job of continuing professional development at the school district's expense. Multiple opportunities were provided to learn many wonderful strategies, from pedagogy to real hands on strategies that made a huge difference in students' learning and in teaching. The test scores and the success of the students demonstrated that the skills that were learned had a direct impact on their success.

The school district had an entire department whose sole focus was to train and support teachers. There was specialized training offered for beginning teachers as well as great learning opportunities for more veteran teachers. Due to budget cuts though, that department shriveled up and eventually died after being active, viable, and user friendly for at least ten years of my teaching career before it went away.

What about the teachers in smaller districts who never had such opportunities to start with? And, what about the teachers who came afterward? There are unfortunately not many options for professional development endeavors that are not too costly either in the monetary cost or in the cost of time taken away from the classroom. There are conferences, but again, the registration cost is high, they are often out of state and require travel (at the teachers' expense), and often are not approved by their administration due to the cost of substitute teachers to replace the teachers while they are gone.

Case in point: In one school district, teachers were rewarded for good attendance on their part (it was part of the package that determined their raises at the end of the year). Yet, that same school district would count a teacher's attendance at a conference against a teacher's overall perfect attendance—even if the teacher was paying for it themselves. Why would any teacher even go? Teachers were expected to go to the conferences and workshops at their own expense and at the risk of losing a potential raise at the end of the school year.

Upon starting at this new school district as a principal I was shocked by the lack of professional development provided to teachers. New teachers were not utilizing relevant pedagogies that had been around for years! It seemed so unbelievable that after so many years this group of teachers did not know or had not even heard about them.

Their lack of knowledge shocked me. Proven, research-supported practices learned and used effectively years ago in the classroom less than twenty miles from where we now were, were foreign concepts to these teachers. There was such a sense of utter disbelief that language that was newer (less than ten years old) but now accepted knowledge as to how to utilize data, measure learning of students, and track growth, were for all intent and purpose, a foreign language to these teachers. How could this be?

Yet, there are schools and teachers to this day who are teaching using methodologies and curriculum that are outdated and not aligned to the standards, but they are still using them and are not aware that they are so outdated. Through research into practices as a new principal, it was discovered that there were classes being taught which were not aligned with the state standards or the descriptions as outlined by the board of education and credits being awarded that, again, were not aligned or even accurate.

Yet, it was happening, and without question we can dare say it is happening in many schools right now. This guarantee is true. It will not matter where you go, name any school from as far west to as far east, from the north to the south and you will find:

1. Schools that are teaching with outdated, unsuccessful teaching strategies.
2. Schools that are using outdated (if any) tools to measure student data and success.
3. Schools that have teachers teaching classes and credits being awarded for those classes that they are not licensed to teach (especially true in smaller schools, charter schools, and private schools).
4. Schools that are offering classes for credits that are not aligned with the state recommendation or are not aligned with the state descriptions.
5. Schools that are being led by administrators who are not current in the most up-to-date laws required by their state to govern their schools.
6. Schools that are producing transcripts that do not fulfill the state minimums for graduation or for the state requirements for the various types of diplomas.
7. Schools that are using in-house professional development (if any at all) due to the lack of funds and their inability to afford training teachers on the newest proven methodologies to enhance learning for students.

These are just a few of the examples that could be offered to you to support the point that is being made of how important continued professional development and remaining current on the trends are to the success and vitality of a teacher—and ultimately to their students and students' families. All of the above listed atrocities (and countless others) are not the result of mean-spirited, ill-intentioned educators. They are due to educators who are so busy teaching and dealing with the day-to-day workings of a classroom that there is neither the time nor the resources to put effort into the research necessary to remain 100 percent current in their fields, so they don't, and students suffer.

What we end up with, is a world of teachers who were trained ten, twenty, or even thirty, or more, years ago who have no new tools to teach this new generation of students. Remember, for those who have been in education for more than a year, some of what they did learn in their college is now outdated with no system to update it.

We, as a society, would be appalled if the doctor who was going to perform our surgery was utilizing outdated forms of surgical techniques and tools. We would come unglued if our anesthesiologist was still using the same gas mask technology to put us under for surgery as he did years ago—even though it was quite effective. The hospital performing such archaic and outdated practices would never remain open, yet we allow our teachers to teach just the same way they learned many years ago with no current training on new, proven methodologies, and yet we, as a society wonder why schools are in trouble.

So, how do we fix this gaping hole? How do we provide professional development for our educators that is meaningful, cost effective, and consistent enough to effect change in our schools? The answer is one that will require, for some, an out-of-the box way of thinking. It will force us to reevaluate class time for our students, how we pay our teachers, and how much we value the currency of our teachers.

You see, in order to make strides in this area, we have to agree that providing professional development for teachers is vital. Let me move forward with some thoughts assuming that we, as a civilized, intelligent society, believe that we must, just as we do in any profession, continue to train our teachers. With that being said, there are some pretty easy solutions if we just start to think differently.

1. We must provide time for our teachers to learn during their work day. That means that we will have to release students from school at least twice a month so that teachers can have time to work together, evaluate data, measure methodology, and plan for success. We must allow our teachers enough time to do that—even at the inconvenience of parents and other stakeholders.
2. We must limit professional development time to looking at instructional practices and not to management issues. Most management issues can be dealt with in an e-mail or a memo and do not require putting all teachers together while dismissing students to do so. We can even prepare a video all teachers can watch to allow the management materials to be more easily and quickly disseminated.

3. We must have clear and consistent intentions regarding what each facility needs for professional development based on where they are, where they need to be, and how they are going to get there. Professional development must be data driven, based on schools' individual needs rather than on a state or federal cookie-cutter mandate. Professional development must be catered to the schools' specific grade, holes in students' achievement, and contain strategies which will move schools to the next level.
4. We must differentiate professional development for our teachers based on their years of experience both in that building and in education as a whole. Professional development is not, and cannot be a one-size-fits-all approach when it comes to teachers, and it must be differentiated to push those who are ready to be pushed while supporting others who are new and need support.
5. We should consider professional development outside of our school districts. Getting a room full of high school English teachers together at one directed, productive meeting in the afternoon is far more beneficial than one or two English teachers sitting together, stumped about how to assist their students in doing better.
6. We need to look at opportunities in our schools for professional development in which we come together and share best practices and what is working in our classrooms. Learning from the best is nothing but beneficial to our students.
7. Finally, we must continue to be clear, concise, consistent, and intentional with professional development for our teachers. We must look at long-range plans rather than this year's newest buzz words, which will be replaced next year.

Curtain #11

Teaching is All About the Heart

Not every person should teach, and not everyone can teach. That is not meant to hurt the feelings of anyone who is, or who is considering being, a teacher or to make any other statement other than that teaching is not for everyone. Teaching is not a fall back profession when everything else in your life did not seem to work out so you decide, "Well I guess I can teach." Teaching is a calling!

Teaching is a life's work! Teaching is and will always be about the heart. Teaching has to begin with the heart and with that innate knowledge that it is above everything else we have talked about thus far and everything that we will talk about later in this book. Successful teachers have the heart for teaching.

Teachers are born; they are not made. Teaching is a calling and one that is almost a mission rather than a career. It is the most thankless, unmaterialistic, giving profession. Understood, spoken by a teacher. But, this is asked of you: How many of us today, when asked, can come up with the name of a great teacher? You know, that teacher, who in some way, in some manner, made a difference in your life; that teacher who you will never forget; that teacher who had an impact on your life, and one whose name you can still remember; that teacher who taught you a life lesson (whether you needed it or not) and that lesson remains with you today; that teacher who you still quote whenever a certain situation in life occurs. Some can come up with a few. Go ahead, pause right now, and come up with the names of at least two teachers who were instrumental in a positive way in your life (insert *Jeopardy* music here).

Come on you are humming it, too. Okay, got those names? Now answer this: Did you ever tell them? Did they know? How? Have you ever written a note to tell them so? Have you expressed that gratitude to them? For most, the answer is no. For a few, the answer is yes.

As every teacher does, we have kept every note written to us on a napkin, typed out on paper, or in a card telling us what a difference we made as a teacher in our students' lives. Each and every one of them are still with us. Every teacher has one of those files/boxes/crates somewhere right now, and they are smiling because they know what I am talking about. They, too, have saved every note, smiled at every card, and read every e-mail sent to them from former students. But, let's go back to the reality that most of us never told any of the teachers that we just thought about and listed in our minds a minute ago while the *Jeopardy* music was playing in our heads, how we felt. Did we?

That's okay, your teachers already know. Where? In their hearts. Because in every great teacher exists a heart that is content in knowing that they taught you something. Your notes, your napkins, your cards, your e-mails, and your letters, no matter how many or how few, are fabulous, but knowing is what really matters, to their heart.

No one enters the teaching career for the money, and no teacher, dare I say, wonders of about an evening when they will invest their millions earned from being a teacher. Many teachers work outside of their profession to subsidize their pay . . . or lack thereof. It is not uncommon to see a teacher tutor, work at a local restaurant, or work elsewhere on weekends, time off of school, or in the summer to make ends meet.

In many states and districts, depending on the family size, the pay for teachers is at, or very near, the poverty level. This is not being said to spark a huge debate about teachers' pay, or lack thereof, but rather to set the reality of it. Most teachers have decorated their entire classrooms as well as purchased all of the supplies for our children to learn at their own expense. And, again, remember what they are making.

They are taking what they make and spending money for our children to be successful in their classroom. If, as a teacher, they are asking for donations for the classrooms at the start of the year, it is only to assist in keeping their costs down realizing two things: many won't or can't donate at all, and the donated material will probably only last until Christmas break, if they are lucky. So why do they do it? Heart!

Seeing great teachers cry at the lack of success of their students is something witnessed by administrators and colleagues so many times. They have learned on their own, sought out resources on their own, asked for help on their own to make their classrooms better on their own. As a young teacher one night, while grading a set of tests that I had felt confident my students were prepared for, I was overwhelmed by sadness when test after test did not reflect the preparation that I had felt so confident in.

I felt pain in my heart regarding what was done and what could have been done differently to prepare my students for the test. The pain and anguish led me to the Internet and to other colleagues to research different ways for reteaching the material so that my students could understand it. Each and every year, every lesson, every assessment is measured by good teachers and they are losing sleep and worrying far more than any parent or student can understand. Why? Because of their hearts. So, before going any further or saying anything else let's make this perfectly clear. Any good teacher has a great heart.

We, therefore, as a society, must demand that our teachers are in their profession for the heart. Not because they "fell back" on teaching or because they "decided why not." Teaching, at its very core, is all about the heart, and we must demand that our teachers' focus be from the heart, for the heart, and to the heart.

Curtain #12

We Must Measure Our Teachers

Just as there is confusion as to what should be taught, when it should be taught, and how it should be measured, there is often confusion as to what "good" teaching is. That is so difficult because passion and heart, which are at the core of what teaching is, are difficult qualities to measure.

How do you measure how much someone cares? How can you know how much passion a teacher has in them for teaching? The real question is, can passion and heart ever effectively be measured? While few would debate that passion and heart cannot be measured, we must then agree on what can be measured in a classroom. For years, this has been a debate. The debate has been over one fundamental question: How can you measure what a teacher teaches and, therefore, what a child learns?

And to that end, what defines a good teacher? Is "good" teaching defined by what is taught or in what is learned? Is "good" teaching something that can even be measured? And, if it can be measured, by what tools and by what criteria? Who will decide what is measured and how it will be measured? After all, if a classroom is successful, then students are learning. Let's just all agree to agree on that.

But, the question becomes, by whose standard of learning and how is that defined? By a state test? And, if we are measuring a teacher's "success" in the classroom by one assessment, any assessment, are we really measuring all of what is happening in the classroom by that teacher? How can all of the other "non-measurable" things that a great teacher does each and every day in his or her classroom be measured?

Many of our colleagues in the business world have been doing this for years. (Trust us, everyone in education has heard that argument.) We in education have heard the stories of how, in factories, if you do not produce you are not rewarded. Or, how in sales, if you do not sell enough, you are not paid well. Or, even in law or in medicine that if you lose a case or a patient dies, you are not compensated as well.

Even as anyone spews that garbage at us as educators, no educator believes it. Any good educator would contend that students are not produce; they cannot be sold, and they cannot be compared to a law case or a medical case. The argument from educators would insist that each student comes to us with unique skills, unique talents, unique challenges, and unique gifts. They are not produced, nor can they be replicated. They are individuals, and therefore, the teaching itself is individualistic and cannot be measured.

Some students come to school prepared to learn; others come to school hungry and beaten (both physically and mentally). Some students, many educators would say, come to school prepared, dressed, and with proper supplies. Others come to school hungry, dirty, and with nothing. Some students return home to a loving environment with a parent, or even two if they are lucky, with whom to eat dinner and be nurtured and encouraged by to do their homework and go to bed at a good hour. While others return home to cook dinner, care for a younger sibling, or fend for themselves, while the parent either works or is just not there.

These arguments have been heard ad nauseam and we will continue to contradict them as educators as long as they continue to muddy the waters of the real issues at hand.

Yet, we must start somewhere and look at something to measure. We must address the issues at hand. So, it really comes down to two issues.

1. Should teaching be measured at all?
2. If teaching itself should indeed be measured, then how and with what measurement?

Let's tackle the first question because it is where the last few years have been spent. There are teachers who would argue that they should not be held accountable for what a student learns due to the many uncontrollable and variable factors that can hamper or enhance a child's learning. Take for example the child who comes to school hungry, abused, or with a myriad of other issues that a school cannot possibly tackle alone. Should a teacher be judged by that student's learning?

Or what about tests (which we will address in another chapter) whose materials a teacher may or may not have much knowledge of. Should a teacher be held to that student's learning? Or, what about the teacher teaching a subject for the first time (or better yet one that they are not licensed to teach). Should a teacher be held to a student's learning that subject?

Again, this could go on and on but the point still remains, for years we, as teachers, have gotten stuck in this mud so far that, in reality, teachers have been held to very little for accountability. It is certain to me that that last statement will ruffle many feathers, but it is true. Teachers, for the most part, are not held to, and their pay not at all reflected by, what happens in their classroom. Teaching is one of the few careers in which how well or how horribly their students learn in their classroom has little relevance to the teacher keeping their job, getting their raise at the end of the year, or repeating the same thing next year and for years to come.

So I will pause here to tell you a personal story from teaching that almost every teacher has experienced. For years and years, as a classroom teacher, there were the expected "evaluations." There were administrators who came into the classroom and "observed" me teach. Those observations and evaluations utilized a plethora of various techniques and strategies. Some years those evaluations consisted of administrators visiting my classroom who would script me verbatim. In other years, as a teacher, administrators would conduct classroom walk-throughs (brief, five-minute visits).

Some years, as a teacher, no administrator was ever seen in my classroom at all, but placed a glowing evaluation in my mailbox, asking me to sign that evaluation, and return that evaluation to them as documentation that it was received. At the end of the day, how well my students were achieving, the data from my classrooms, the methodologies utilized by me to teach, and ultimately the evaluation received by me (if at all) would have no bearing on the fact that there was an achievement of another year of experience, and therefore, I would have a raise next year. Some years, during my teaching career, there was no evaluation at all as it was not my "turn" on the evaluation rotation schedule.

Let's pause here and let that last thought resonate. There was a confidence, for many, in knowing that teaching was something done well. There was never a question in many of my colleagues' minds in regard to our doing their best for their students each and every day. As a teacher, every opportunity was sought out by us to try to learn from others and ask questions, but sometimes for a few years in a row, there would be no evaluation of us at all.

No one came into the classroom for an *entire school year* and saw what teaching was happening in classrooms, how teaching was happening in classrooms, or if effective teaching was happening at all. It would give me great pleasure to tell you that this lack of evaluation and observation was a rarity to the profession, but sadly it is not. For many teachers, early in their career a category was given to them as a "good" teacher, and therefore, they were just left to fend for themselves. There were no suggestions in an evaluation as to how to get better, but their pay was increased at the end of the year, year after year, because "there was another year of experience" but nothing more.

Nothing earned that raise. Each year as improvements were made personally in teaching, they were made by choice, but not because there was a great need to get better required by the evaluation. There was no growth professionally as a result of evaluations. There was not accountability to the learning of the students, nor was their learning measured by the evaluation. There was no accountability to the behaviors of the students as long as a minimum number of referrals went to the office and the students were kept in their classrooms, behaving and "learning."

There were no evaluations by the administration as to what the parents of the students thought as long as none of the students' parents were calling the office and complaining about the teacher. This is shameful, but without question for far too many teachers, this experience is common and ongoing. So, it is not surprising, why so many teachers (especially veteran teachers who were under that old system) are screaming from the rooftops about the new evaluation system and the possibility of merit pay.

In summation, let me be very clear. For many teachers, raises happen at the end of every school year regardless of their performance on the job. Now, make no mistakes, teaching is something that is in the blood. For many there was a feeling of deserving those raises, but the evaluations as a good teacher existed in our own opinions and by our own comparisons of each other. The definition of "good" teacher was defined as coming to work on time, teaching classes, keeping students learning and engaged (by individual standards), and keeping under the radar of administrators. Is that enough?

For a long time, the profession has hung onto the "should" of measuring good teaching. We, in many states, are moving past that. There is no question about all of the "unmeasurables" of teaching. There is also a complete understanding of the vast difference in how evaluating teachers has come from practically nothing, more or less, to a whole new rubric with real teeth and bite.

But, not being able to measure all aspects of teaching cannot hold us back from measuring the many aspects of teaching that we can measure. There are proven data and proven, researched strategies and methods that are being used in highly successful classrooms across the world. There are data and research to support certain qualitative techniques that result in high student learning and high student achievement.

We must, as a profession, look at those and measure them. We do not all have to agree on all of them, but we have to uncross our arms, pull back our pouting lips, get out of our old archaic manner of evaluations, and quit saying, "But I teach children; how can you measure that?" We must, as a society demand that every teacher, whether they agree or not, like it or not, or want it or not, be utilizing the newest strategies that have been data tested and proven to work in enhancing student learning.

We have to get out of our own way, as educators, and realize that the students of today are demanding a new manner of learning and we must adapt if we do not want to continue as a society being left in the dust by other countries when it comes to educational advancements. So, once we move past the "should we" to the how, we can grow together.

The second question becomes one of how. How do we measure good teaching?

The above paragraphs should in no way suggest that there are not good teachers. In many states, we have developed a rubric to measure "good." Well, we in the business of education do not say "good" or "bad"; we say ineffective, needs improvement, effective, and highly effective. We have put together a rubric with many competencies to "measure" what teaching looks like and where on a scale teachers are placed so that we can adjust their pay accordingly.

Some would argue that the rubric has been shoved down the throats of educators, but let me tell you what most teachers will not tell you. Good teachers are not threatened by this new rubric. Good teachers who want the best for their students and who are willing to learn, grow, and be held to a standard that every other teacher is being held to are not threatened or bothered by this new evaluation system.

Sure, most of these teachers will not say that out loud for fear of the public flogging from their more veteran colleagues who are absolutely outraged that they are even being measured at all. They will sit quietly and watch their colleagues petition at their local governmental offices or house politicians even speaking about this latest evaluative tool. They will watch quietly, not at all threatened by this new tool, because they know they are good at their craft and they are not threatened by any tool that will measure how good they are. They are more concerned and interested in the facets of the tool and how it can become the best and most effective tool to use rather than arguing over the silliness of if there should even be a tool at all.

In many states, we have finally begun to move forward with at least a common language in a rubric that will measure what is happening (or not happening) in the classrooms across our states and throughout the country. There has been a huge upheaval as the "rubric," or many versions of it, has become law in my state, and in countless others. There have been teachers screaming and yelling and petitioning and protesting from the rooftops that good teachers cannot be measured.

Again, remember who was just outlined as doing the screaming and the yelling. To those educators please hear this, come out from behind your protected classroom door where you have hidden for years and come into the real world. No other profession with as high stakes as we have in education allows the very people who do it to not be measured. No one in their right mind would allow anyone in front of their child to teach them, understanding that they are not being held to some agreed upon *minimum* standard, whatever that may be. And as educators, neither can we.

We have to quit fighting, arguing, and screaming that we, as a profession, cannot be measured because of what we do. We have to quit acting as if what we do is a profession that is above measurement and evaluation because of the students that we serve. We cannot continue to think that way. Yes, we can be measured, and yes we must be measured.

How dare we, as educators, claim so unjustly that we cannot be held to the same standard of a meaningful evaluation that every other worker and employee in any other work of life is held to. Who are we? What makes us immune? We simply cannot do it anymore. We, as educators, both new and those of us who have built our careers in education, must work together to ensure that the tool itself is the best tool possible and abandon the outdated, unrealistic, archaic argument that there should not even be a tool at all.

As a society, we must continue to work together to redefine, readjust, and continually monitor the tool that is used to measure good teaching, but we must move past the argument that there is no need for a tool at all. What every good educator knows but will never say out loud is this truth.

As long as we continue to argue about what the tool looks like, how it will be used, if it should be used, how teachers will be measured, when teachers will be measured, and of course, if they should be measured at all, teachers know they will continue to muddy the political waters so much that they can continue, as they have for decades, to not really be meaningfully measured or held accountable at all.

Teachers, and their unions, are very savvy and know that as long as we keep the public arguing over this tool, what it will look like, and if it can be used, we will continue to not be held accountable to it. And, for many states, that is working. The back and forth arguments regarding every period, comma, and word on that rubric or evaluation measurement tool carry on and nothing changes in too many classrooms. Due to this political maneuvering, too many teachers continue to teach in classrooms today utilizing the same archaic methodologies that they learned years and years ago and are able to continue to use. And, again we wonder why our system is broken.

Let's have an example of this from the administrator's chair. When I first became a principal, my state had mandated by law that all teachers must be measured by some form of a rubric that had been created. The schools had a few years to be in compliance, but my school district decided to jump right in and get started. What was being said by teachers was appalling.

Teachers were arguing over every word and every point on that rubric. They were incensed that a rubric and their performance in the classroom could impact their pay. There was a sheer sense of disbelief that what they did in the classroom every day could possibly be tied to the amount of their paycheck every other Friday. Hearing some of this come out of the mouths of intelligent, college educated people was jaw-dropping.

What the teachers often heard from the principal's chair was, "How can we, as teachers, not be held to the same standard that every other working American (or human) is held to?" "How can we as teachers not be held accountable on what students are learning in our classrooms?" Many teachers would just look as if what was being asked was the most ridiculous question they had ever heard and respond by saying, "Because we are teachers. We teach students and each student is different. We cannot be held, and should not be held, to what they learn and when they learn it."

Yes, folks, that is what almost every teacher will say. Yes, no kidding, and yes, that is why we are where we are in establishing a tool and utilizing it. Again, this is the dirty little secret that most will not tell you, but sadly, shameful as it is to say, it is true. The rebuttal to them would be, "Come on folks. You cannot surely think that. I for one was a great teacher and we all knew 'that teacher' who, because they had more experience, was making more money, and who we all knew was not a good teacher."

The defense would continue: "Come on. I for one, would have loved merit pay as a teacher. I was a good teacher, my students achieved, and I would have made more money early on." Again, the teachers would look at me and say, "Yes, but . . ." and continue on with lists such as these:

- What if you have a bad administrator who just does not like you?
- What if you have a student who comes to you unprepared to be in your class? That is not your fault.
- What if, even after you teach, the student just does not learn? That should not be the teacher's fault. Right?
- What if a child refuses to learn?
- What if the student does not come to school or their attendance is bad?
- What if the parents do not make them come to school prepared with their homework?
- What if the school system does not like you?
- What if the teacher who had the student in the level or grade before you did not prepare them so they are not as prepared as they should be? That should not be the current teacher's fault, right?
- What about students with special needs? They should not count against you. Right?
- What about students who are removed from school for discipline issues? They should not count. Right?
- What about students who transfer into your classroom mid-year or mid-semester? You are not responsible for them, correct?
- What about if you don't have the materials you want or need? Then you can't teach the students, right?
- What about the political revision of the rubric over the years? Teachers should not be held to a rubric that is still in the works or not completely set yet, right?
- What about classroom standards that have been changed on a teacher mid-year?

Again, this could keep going and going, and yes, as an administrator each and every one of those questions above comes right out of the mouths of colleagues and go straight to the heart. So, you can see why we are where we are in the evaluation system. Nowhere. We, as a profession, have learned the art of arguing to stop the process.

There are some states that are further along in the process of creating this rubric and other states that have decided that evaluating teachers and utilizing one rubric to hold all teachers to the same criteria is just too political to touch and have let it go. So, as teachers continue to argue and politicians continue to either dance around the issue or confront the continued attack, the students in our classrooms are caught in the crossfire.

Our students are left with teachers held to no standard—year after year. Let that thought resonate with you for a moment. Year after year, while we as adults argue, fight, reword, evaluate, and complain about how and with what tools teachers should be measured, students are left in the dust. There should be no question why this system is broken.

But what about the schools that do have a tool and are evaluating teachers? That is good, right? Well, think about this. What we have in our state and in many others now is a tool—a rubric, albeit one in various forms that "measures" what is good teaching. This rubric now must be used in every school system throughout this state and many others. This rubric has a point value and that point value, along with other measurable items such as teacher attendance, professional development, and a myriad of other measureable criteria, now defines not only what a teacher's pay raise will be at the end of the school year, but when they will get that pay raise.

This rubric has been riddled by political maneuvering, petitioning, and division as has never been seen in this profession. It is considered, as an educator, almost blasphemy to agree with the rubric and to state that you are okay with the use of it. Well folks, that blasphemy has been coming out of my mouth ever since this rubric started. What I have said and will continue to say about the rubric used in this state is this: There is agreement that our current rubric is not perfect and that it may need tweaking and modification. *At least we finally have one.* At least, while perhaps not perfect, we have finally moved from the question of *should* teachers be measured at all to some common agreed upon language that we can build on and grow. We have moved into a rubric that, like it or not, has us all beginning to use a common language and understand teaching expectations.

We are starting to gear professional development in a manner that moves toward the data we are now utilizing. We are starting conversations that are centered on student learning rather than what teachers teach. We are moving in the right direction. As political maneuvering attempting to stop it continues, there is faith that we will not go backward, but will move forward in refining the tool that we currently have. Let me give you a case in point of how great this rubric has been in the few short years it has been in existence for me as an administrator.

In one of our buildings, there was a teacher whose teaching was less than effective. Her test scores were dismal, her state testing scores were the lowest in the county, students were out of control in her classroom, and students were not learning and everyone knew it.

It took three years, much legal maneuvering, and being on the "stand" with the school board for over nine hours to have her removed. Year one, she was put on an improvement plan; year two she continued on the improvement plan with weekly meetings and observations. Year three, countless meetings with the union, with her lawyer, with the superintendent, and with the school board, and she was allowed to resign at the end of the school year.

All three years she still taught students, still had dismal test results, and students still failed the state test under her. Think of the amount of students who were impacted. Think of the students that were allowed to be "educated" in her classroom when every administrator, and many teachers, knew she was not effective in her teaching and students were not learning.

Fast forward to a new district using the new evaluation rubric. Another teacher was not being effective in his classroom. Students were not learning based on the weekly data we were measuring (teacher and administrator together), and the classroom was out of control. Yet, here is the new process. After semester one observations, numbers on the rubric support the documentations of ineffective teaching for this teacher.

Therefore, semester two, the teacher and evaluator met weekly to address lessons, student learning, data in the classroom, and behavioral issues (many times the teacher includes his representative in that meeting). After mid-way through the second semester and with no growth noted, the teacher was allowed to resign at the end of the school year.

Note the time difference—from three years to one year. Note the time difference and the reduction in the number of students adversely affected. There is no suggestion that the rubric has been created and should be used for firing teachers, but there is no concern either, nor should there be for any good teacher, with a rubric that removes ineffective teachers who are hurting students.

We must as a society demand that our teachers be held to the same criteria as any other employee. We must hold every teacher and every administrator to a rubric that measures student learning and student success. We must continue to put students' learning above adults' needs and stay at the forefront of what happens in the classroom and what is measured.

Curtain #13

There Are "Bad" Teachers

I have dreaded raising this curtain. Every educator who is in any school across the United States knows it is true. Every parent who has ever had a student go through a school system knows it is true.

> *And here it is:* There are bad teachers in our schools, right now, teaching students. *There are teachers who have no clue how to teach, who really do not want to teach, and who are not serving their students, right now. As you are reading this, there are classrooms of students being "taught" by what every teacher knows is a bad teacher.*

Before the topic of the "why" can be discussed, let's agree on the definition of "bad." "Bad" in its very sense is not beneficial, nor is it measureable. "Bad" is in the eye of the beholder. It is like "good," or "pretty," or "ugly" and is tough to measure. So, for the sake of clarity, in this chapter, let's define "bad" as such: On most teacher evaluation measurement systems, regardless of what tool is being used, there is a category that measures a teacher as below standards, or unsatisfactory.

There again are a myriad of words and competencies used to label that teacher, but for the purpose of this section of the book we will agree that "bad" is defined as meeting the lowest standard set by the school system in the majority of the competencies.

If you ask any teacher to name a "bad" teacher in their building right now, they know of one, maybe more. Ask any administrator if they have a "bad" teacher in their buildings right now. If they are being honest, they will say yes. Now, whether or not they will give up the name of that "bad" teacher depends on who you are and why you are asking, and if they think that information will ever get back to that teacher whose name they could give you.

It is shameful that we must admit this about our educators. It is embarrassing to admit that even when I was a student, a student teacher, and when I was a principal, this was a common fact. As a union representative, there were times while I was "protecting their rights" that I felt as though I was bathing in disgust at the lack of a teacher's teaching skills and their ability to prepare students appropriately.

It is infuriating that in a profession that is "all about the students," we allow teachers who are not effective to remain in classrooms year after year. So, the question is why? Why is it happening? And, why are we allowing it?

Well, there are many reasons for it happening. Most of them are excuses, but they are our truths in education. So, here are some of the most embarrassing things first-hand knowledge can share. Remember, the position of union representative meant that I "defended" some colleagues, but as an assistant principal I witnessed much of this from a different perspective.

I heard about bad teachers from the principal's chair, from colleagues, from the superintendent's chair to the teacher's desk and all steps in-between—it is all the same—I even overheared parents having those discussions in the bleachers and in the stands of various activities. Everyone knows that there are "bad" teachers, but what many do not know is why.

Why are "bad" teachers allowed to be in our classrooms? The answer to that is long and has many layers, so sit back for this exposé of the layers of this stinky onion as I have only ever shared it with a very few. Sit back as this one will smell; it is an embarrassing truth for every educator who has spent more than a week inside any classroom across our great nation.

The solution exists in fixing each of the parts that is being outlined. The solution to removing the "bad" teachers from our classrooms resides in all of us as we read this, demand action, and work together toward the solution.

Curtain #14

How We Measure "Bad" Teachers

Many of the "bad" teachers are still in classrooms today due to a lack of measurement tools that really define what "bad" teaching is.

Let's not reiterate that part of this book which discusses the rubric (or any other measuring tool) or the lack thereof, but for many "bad" teachers that lack of clear measurement tools is the issue preventing their removal from the classroom. They have slipped by year after year because no clear tool, and therefore no clear expectations of what "good" is, has been defined. As there is no tool, there is no manner in which to measure them as "bad"; therefore, they remain.

Year after year they remain in the classroom caught in a limbo of what "bad" teaching is as defined by the administrator at the time. And, far too often, teachers will outlast their administration, so as the administration changes, the process that may or may not have begun to remove that "bad" teacher, will start all over again. I have heard colleagues say, "'Blank' principal tried to get rid of me and now she is gone. That is the third principal that has tried to get rid of me, and I am still here." And, they are.

So, if there is no clear sense of what "bad" teaching is, the teacher remains. Again, as has been stated above, until schools become clear on what qualities and expectations define "good" teaching and recognize that those qualities and practices are important to teaching as a skill, "bad" teachers will continue to be in our schools.

Curtain #15

Even "Bad" Teachers Are Members of Our Communities

This is the toughest part about removing "bad" teachers. Teachers are far more than teachers.

For most of us, teachers are more than that person who taught us math, science, history, or English. They are a mentor: they offered guidance, that beacon of hope, that listening ear, they were that hero that you look up to. They are the person who listened to you when you broke up with your boyfriend. They were that ear the year you had them for history and your parents divorced.

They were that coach who not only taught you science but who helped you discover the basketball player in you, and that knowledge of basketball has landed you a full scholarship to college. They are far more than your English teacher, but the person who stayed with you after school to help you learn English better, because your parents did not speak English at home.

There is story after story in the papers, on the news, in books and in various other print and Internet publications of amazing men and women who have had a profound effect on countless children's lives. How can that coach, that mentor, that listener, or that person be a "bad" teacher? They were not a "bad" teacher to you, to your son, or to your daughter. And therein lies the issue. You see, teaching at its very core is personal.

To take students who, no matter what grade they are in, are positively influenced by their teachers and then measure those teachers as "bad" is not acceptable to us. Parents become outraged that their favorite coach who helped their son get into college is getting a bad evaluation. How can this be? How can the teacher that listened to that student going through the divorce of her parents be a "bad" teacher?

You see in order for a teacher to be effective they must build relationships with their students, but it is often those relationships with their students that muddy the waters and prevent us from being able to measure teachers. The waters have become so muddied that sometimes the very thing that is a strength for teachers, forming great relationships with their students, is the very thing that keeps their students from learning.

It is in being the students' "friends" that clouds the ability, for many, to teach. It is almost impossible to separate the teacher as a person who must form relationships with their students from the teacher as an employee with the craft and skills necessary to instruct those students. And what makes the waters even muddier is that what defines a teacher as either "good" or "bad" is often subjective (student and parent). The relationship of a student or parent to a teacher often depends on the teacher's personality and how well it aligns with the student or parent.

Let me pause for a moment to clarify that, when speaking about the relationships between students and their teachers, I am not referring to any relationship that is illegal or unethical. The countless court cases of teachers "crossing the line" in their inappropriate relationships with their students will not be addressed. Those are not the relationships that are being spoken of here.

Remember, most teachers are great teachers. They form amazing relationships with their students and it is through those relationships that students learn. In many situations, students will spend more hours per day with their teachers than with their parents. Think about that fact for a moment. For far too many students, the largest impact and impression made on them is not made by their parents; it is made by their teachers. If we look at just the sheer amount of hours students are spending at home and at school, it is the volume of time at school and the relationships with their teachers that have the greatest impact.

Putting that oldest daughter on the bus for the first time and sending her off to kindergarten comes with mixed emotions. By the time that the first one goes off to school, a teaching career was ten years underway. As if it were yesterday, I remember standing at that bus and thinking about that; for the first time in my daughter's life, ever since the day we brought her home from the hospital, we, her parents, had been her most important teachers.

We were the ones, aside from her daycare provider (whom we selected), who were with her the most. We controlled what she learned, when she learned it, who cared for her if it was not her dad or me, who was around her, who spoke to her, what they taught her, how they taught her, and what she was learning. We were now passing much of that to our local public school system.

Though we knew who her teacher was going to be, as in we knew her name, we did not know her. We did not know if she was current on the latest teaching methodologies or if she was successful in teaching kindergarten in the past. We did not know what our daughter would be taught, being only familiar with high school curricula. There was no knowledge about kindergarten curriculum and if our daughter was leaving kindergarten and progressing through the public school system appropriately, but we trusted the relationships that we continued to have with that first kindergarten teacher to the last high school teacher our youngest son had twenty years later.

Thinking of the sheer number of hours that my own children have spent with, and the relationships that they have formed with, their teachers is mind boggling. And, remember too, in my situation, both my husband and I remained active in the relationships that our children had with their teachers. We had the dinner conversations about their teachers and the relationships they had with them. As a teacher familiar with "the business," parent conferences happened with the parent and teacher speaking the same language.

I had first-hand knowledge that the relationships between teachers and students were vital to students' success in their classrooms, so I completely understood the importance of such relationships. For too many students, teachers are the parents to their students. In later chapters, I will address student and parent perspectives, but the point here is the uncomfortableness of trying to separate the relationship of a teacher and student from the "craft" or "skills" in delivering good instruction.

We all know that teachers provide students with far more instruction on a daily basis than parents often do. With all of that "relationships part," it is hard to remove "bad" teachers, because the heart is at stake. It is hard to imagine that the great guy that coaches your son's little league team is being fired for being a bad teacher. He is such a great guy. Or, that wonderful woman who took your child home every Tuesday because you were working two jobs is receiving a bad evaluation. Or, that the selfless man who bought your son a suit because your husband had passed away and you had no money to buy him one is being put on an improvement plan because his students are not achieving well on the state test. Adults become outraged. You see, relationships are vital for good teachers to teach. But, it is often those very relationships that can, and often do, make it impossible to remove "bad" teachers. It is hard for anyone who is not in the business of education to understand that teaching is more than the relationships. Relationships are vital and important, but they are not the end all and be all that determine whether a teacher should remain in a school.

We have to remove that piece, relationships, as a determining factor in our evaluations of teachers. We have to remember that forming great relationships with students is *one*, albeit a very important one, tool for successful teaching. Being a good person and forming good relationships with students cannot be the only measure of good teaching.

Curtain #16

The "Untouchables"

There will not be as much said as could be in regards to this topic, as it would cloud the entire book. Going too far into this topic might cause the purpose of the entire book to be lost, but removing a "bad" teacher becomes much more difficult if that teacher is a coach. It is even tougher if they are a coach and they have either:

1. Had winning seasons.
2. Been in the community for quite some time.
3. Had a parent who also was a coach in the same school district.

> *There are those in education who we refer to as "the untouchables." Coaches, especially effective or winning coaches, are at the top of that list, and removing them from a classroom is difficult, to say the least.*

If you are a coach, have had successful season(s), are well liked in the community, and have a history at your school, then you are an "untouchable." So, who is an "untouchable" you ask? They are men or women who, regardless of effectiveness *in* their classrooms on a daily basis, cannot be fired. They are immune to bad evaluations and any principal who dares to go against an "untouchable" will be run out of their building. The value they have to that school district is not in their teaching, but in their coaching and the continued success they are having in that sport.

If you want to test me, do this: Ask any student right now to come up with the name of a good coach, one that is successful and well-liked, who they had as a teacher. Ask them if they learned much in the classroom, and, in many cases, they will laugh and tell you that the teacher/coach talked mostly about their sport and "favored" the athletes. They will tell you that the teacher was often unprepared, lectured, was late returning paperwork, and they, as students, knew the teacher was not doing a good job. But, even as students, they knew the teacher was a well-respected coach and would never lose their job.

Now, let me pause here to say this. In no shape or form is there any implication that every teacher who is a coach is a bad teacher. It has also never been said that because a teacher chooses to coach they cannot be a good teacher. As a matter of fact, the contrary has been observed. I have had the opportunity to see coaches as teachers do quite well in the classroom, but that is not what this section of the book is talking about.

What is being talked about are the "untouchable" coaches who believe their full-time job is to coach a winning season and whatever time they have left over, if any, is devoted to their teaching and preparation for the classroom. Witnessing the following through time and across education has a sobering effect.

- Coaches given lighter teaching loads, especially during their seasons, so that they can have more time to coach.
- Coaches being exempt from professional development expectations or directives especially if they are "in season."
- Coaches being late or not submitting required paperwork and excused for it, especially if they are "in season."
- Coaches, who, despite being paid extra to coach, have less daily responsibilities/duties as compared to their non-coaching colleagues.
- Coaches who have said inappropriate things to students on and off the field and are "disciplined" though remain in the classroom and coaching.
- Coaches who are late to meetings, leave early from meetings, and often do not attend required meetings, especially when they are "in season."

There has always been a double standard when it comes to athletics, and therefore, when it comes to coaches. We see it play out daily in the media and in the professional world of athletics, but make no mistake folks, it begins in our schools. We see it on the larger scale as athletes are held to very different standards than non-athletes. Those behaviors were learned at a young age, in our schools, so it is no wonder that we have a litany of adults with that mentality.

So, why don't administrators discipline these "untouchables"? Let's address that in a moment, but, first, let's just say this: To discipline or "go after" an "untouchable" is political suicide for any administrator. These "untouchables" are often revered in the community. Parents love them, spectators adore watching them, students are getting scholarships due to them, and the stands or fields are full on Friday night bringing in quite a bit of revenue to the school because of them. The truth is, for many, no one cares what is happening in their classroom on Monday as long as the team wins on Friday. As long as the victories keep coming, they are "untouchable."

They are equally as susceptible to the opposite reaction, however, if they begin losing. Start losing and all of a sudden what is happening in the classroom *will* get them fired. There will be such an outcry for their heads on a platter that teacher/coaches will be ousted from their coaching positions and ultimately their teaching positions until they can get to another building and coach; therefore, what you have is a group of teachers in every building across this country who are not good teachers and everyone knows it; but, they are "untouchables" and therefore remain in the classroom "teaching" our children, and we allow it.

The solution is tough. This one is so tough because we must first admit to having the problem. We must be willing to look at all adults in our buildings as valuable, contributing members of our staff. Regardless of what they teach or who they are as people outside of their classroom, they must be valued and measured equally in the classroom. This is a pedagogy that, with certainty, will be a tough hill to climb.

Take a moment and look at the value we place on our professional athletes. There are some that would argue that they can get away with murder—literally. There is a double standard in the manner in which they are often treated by the law, on the streets, in stores, and in the media. It is no wonder that the bigger-than-life persona would translate on a smaller scale to our schools and to our classrooms. The fix will be on a much larger scale, but until it does, the "untouchables" will be teaching your children. Not because they are good teachers but because they are "untouchable."

Curtain #17

Why Are "Bad" Teachers Not Getting Fired?

To the person not in the business, the solution to the question "Why are "bad" teachers not getting fired?" seems so easy. If an administrator knows that a teacher is not being effective, why don't they get fired? Or, if year after year a teacher has students who do not perform well on state tests and everyone knows it, why does the teacher not get fired? It seems like such a "duh" question that so many outside of education cannot understand why it is happening in our schools.

Throughout my time in education, I have had friends who have told story after story of employees at their companies being called into an office and being dismissed on the spot. The employees were escorted to their desks to remove their personal things and walked, by security, to the front door, where they surrendered their keys and swipe cards. While listening to those stories one should also hear, "That would not happen in a public school system."

It is always perplexing because some of the employees said that they were being let go due to no fault of their own, but due to downsizing or budget cuts. My friends went on to say that the employee themselves did not know the termination/downsizing/removal was coming, and in some instances the employee had received a glowing evaluation just a few months or weeks prior to their being let go. This is a foreign concept in education.

In public school life, there would never have been such an experience with any person being let go so quickly and swiftly as to be escorted out or be called into a meeting in which they did not know they were going to be let go. That is not a world that the public school has ever entered. However, once, while spending six months in the charter school world, I witnessed such an event. There were opportunities in that charter school world to watch and participate in removing bad teachers immediately.

This experience of being let go immediately became personal when I was called to a meeting and let go due to downsizing. I would never have thought of this happening, as just the day before we were discussing plans for moving into the next semester. Though the "cause" for dismissal was labeled budget cuts, the meeting left me with feelings of shock and confusion; I thought, this would have never happened in a public school.

Such a scenario as this was one would never happen in a public school. As a teacher, there was one occurrence in which an administrator was put on "administrative" leave after a legal case outside of the school, but that had nothing to do with her teaching and was completely separate from the classroom from which she was removed.

My response to friends who tell these stories would be that never in thirty years in *public schools* would they have witnessed similar dismissals, of teachers being fired for being bad teachers. This is not a reference to the extreme cases where a teacher has been accused of breaking the law; in those instances, removal is swift. What is being referred to here are examples of the teacher who year after year is a "bad" teacher.

In the public school world, there are four criteria that keep "bad" teachers from being removed. These are not talked about, yet every administrator and every teacher knows what they are. If a teacher wants to remain in their job, they know how to play the game and some have become masterful at doing so.

The impediments to removal are:

1. The time it takes to remove "bad" teachers.
2. The lack of continuity of any administrator to complete the removal process of a "bad" teacher.
3. The lack of an effective tool to measure what "bad" is in regards to that teacher.
4. The political fallout for the administrator who removes a "bad" teacher.

As has been mentioned before, there is a lack of continuity in administration, but here is a more detailed description in explanation of the time it takes to remove a "bad" teacher. Depending on the teacher, the time of the evaluation schedule, the observation rotation that year, and the type of tool that is being used to evaluate that teacher, it can take up to *three years* to remove a "bad" teacher from the classroom. There are many variables that can come into play, but as a general rule of thumb, when any administrator declares that a teacher is "bad" and needs to get better, it can take up to three years from the initial notification to that teacher until the teacher is ultimately terminated. The following example is an extreme case, but such cases occur far too often in our schools today.

- Fall Evaluation—Year One: teacher is informed that their classroom strategies are not up to par and they will need to be put on an improvement plan.
- Spring Evaluation—Year One: teacher is placed on an improvement plan. This plan includes weekly observations and weekly meetings with the administrator who placed them on the improvement plan. Let's, for arguments sake, say that the improvement plan lists three categories that the teacher must improve upon.
- End of Year Evaluation—Year One: gains have been made on one of the goals that were established. Teacher remains on the improvement plan for the next year.
- Fall Opening Evaluation—Year Two: teacher begins the school year on the same improvement plan as last spring. There are still weekly observations and weekly meetings with the administrator who placed the teacher on the improvement plan. Remember, last spring *one* of the goals was achieved, so it has been removed from the plan.
- Fall Final Evaluation—Year Two: teacher has made growth toward one of the two remaining goals, but has not really gotten good enough to call it completed. Plan to keep the improvement plan in place for the next semester.
- Spring Evaluation—Year Two: administrator continues with weekly observations and weekly meetings with the teacher, probably a department chair, and perhaps a union representative now, because the administrator is not seeing growth at the level it needs to be for the two remaining goals.
- Spring End of Year Evaluation—Year Two: meeting is held with the teacher, the union representative, and the administrator reiterating the fact that there has not been growth toward the two remaining goals, and the administration would encourage the teacher's resignation. This is not the first time that this kind of conversation has taken place. This conversation probably began in the fall of year two and has continued, becoming more urgent as lack of growth was observed by the administrator. The union representative, after speaking with the teacher, disagrees and wants another administrator's observation and is fighting the recommendation to resign.
- Fall Evaluation—Year Three: new administrator is meeting weekly with the teacher and the union representative and is conducting weekly observations and weekly coaching meetings. If there is an instructional coach at the building level, he or she has already been brought into the process and is also conducting their weekly meetings apart from the administrative weekly meetings.

- Fall Final Evaluation—Year Three: the new administrator, after weekly observations and weekly meetings has the same findings regarding the lack of movement toward the remaining goals. The teacher and the union representative refuse to agree with the recommendation to resign, and the legal process for removing the teacher begins at Christmas-time of year three. Note here that the administration has been keeping the superintendent apprised of this process thus far. Personnel and the superintendent are already advised of the teacher's status for the past three years, since such notification is common practice.
- Spring Evaluation—Year Three: there is a recommendation to terminate this teacher at the end of the school year. The teacher and their union representative disagree with the decision and want a hearing. All observations and weekly meetings stop as they are deemed to be "harassment." For the next several months, there will be meetings held with a myriad of groups, the teachers, some students (to verify they learned in teachers' class), perhaps parents, administration, union representatives, and the school board. All of this political wrangling has to happen while the school year is still going on.
- Spring End of Year Evaluation—Year Three: after multiple hearings, the school board supports the administration's documentation to remove the teacher. Upon gaining knowledge that the school board is going to support the administration for termination, the teacher resigns and moves on to another school district. The other school district is none the wiser as the teacher states that they "resigned" from their previous school for whatever reason they care to give.

What is probably being said here is, "Come on; that doesn't really happen, does it?" If you are asking that, know this: it does really happen. I have witnessed many such instances of the above scenario. I have experienced such cases from the perspective of a union representative, as an administrator performing observations, and as a principal defending the decision to terminate a teacher. I have never experienced the process from a teacher's perspective, as there was never an occasion for me to be placed on an improvement plan or to be recommended for termination.

Now let's agree to bring some assumptions into play. There is an assumption that throughout this three-year process none of the administrators changed because if any of the administrators changed the process could take much longer, even double the time. There must also be an assumption made that the teacher is not an "untouchable."

Another assumption that must be made is that the teacher does not carry too much political clout in the community as that too can drag the process out even longer; and the final assumption is that everyone involved, from all of the teachers to the administration and the other adults involved, remain quiet to everyone outside of the process, including other parents and other teachers, regarding any step of the process, because, when more people get involved, social media becomes a factor, or the media becomes involved, bringing the entire process to a halt until that source is appeased.

So, let's also look at the time commitment involved to remove a "bad" teacher. Beginning in the fall of year one there were weekly meetings and weekly observations of that teacher. Let's do the math:

> 40 weeks of school x 1 hour weekly observation = 40 hours in observations (per year) + 1 hour each week of past observation meetings = 80 hours in observations (per year) x 3 years = 240 hours
> 240 hours divided by 8 hours a day divided by 4 weeks in a month = *6 WEEKS*

It takes at least *six weeks* to remove a "bad" teacher from a classroom. Think about that, what if there is more than one "bad" teacher? That is not counting the meetings that have taken place along the way with:

- The teacher and an academic coach;
- The teacher and their department chair;
- The administrator and the academic coach;
- The administrator and the respective department chair;
- The administrator and the superintendent (or designee);
- The teacher and the superintendent (or designee);
- The teacher and the union representative;
- The administrator and the union representative;
- The teacher, the administrator, and the union representative;
- The school board and the teacher;
- The school board and the administrator;
- The school board, the superintendent (or designee), and the administrator.

If we were to assume that these meetings listed above happened only once a month, and that is a low estimate, that would be an additional twelve meetings, for eleven months, for one hour (assuming for math purposes), for three years. That is 396 hours divided by eight hours in a work day equals 49.5 days. Divide that by the five days in a work week and we have added another 9.9 weeks. At this moment the school system has spent almost three months over the three years to dismiss a bad teacher.

Are you still questioning why any administrator is not removing a "bad" teacher? This is all assuming that the administrator has kept perfect records of every evaluation, every meeting, and has kept all notes, all suggestions, all improvement plans, all e-mail communications, all notes on those improvement plans, and all notes from every meeting ever held, in a concise, timelined binder to be presented when the teacher is recommended for termination.

Remember this total does not include the hours that this documentation preparation will take the administrator along the way to gather, produce, and present. All administrators know they are facing this daunting task, and frankly, from the time it will take away from the day-to-day running of a building, are just not willing to put in the time.

The other problem is that some administrators lack the follow-through to document all meetings properly or to follow up to complete the task. Any hole, any error, any typo, any missed meeting, any missed observation is a loophole to stop the process and either force it to start over or, ultimately, cause it to fail to terminate the "bad" teacher.

As a building-level principal, hours such as these are not uncommon. Those meetings have been held; those binders have been gathered; those observations have been done; and that massive amount of time has been put in. However, the entire process is disgusting, because, even though everyone knows that the teacher must be removed, the paperwork and the time that it takes to do so, must be taken away from other things that should and need to be done.

Even the teachers watching all of the paperwork, observations, and meetings know that bad teachers must be removed; yet they too, watch and say nothing. This entire process is ridiculous, and there has to be a better method to evaluate teachers and a timelier manner to remove "bad" teachers. Fortunately, as stated in previous chapters, there is recourse in some states, but that is not true of far too many states and, therefore, "bad" teachers remain.

Okay, so what has been addressed is the lack of a good tool, the time that it can take to remove a "bad" teacher, and the issues that can happen to stall or even stop the process if there is a lack of continuity in administration, but what must be addressed is the other *big* white elephant in the room—the political fallout of removing a "bad" teacher.

The final piece to removing a "bad" teacher is the political devastation it will have on the administrator to remove that "bad" teacher. Remember in a previous chapter when the "political sand" that is either put in or taken out of the political cup of every administrator was discussed? Well, depending on who the teacher is, how adversarial the observations and meetings have been, how much talking is done on the part of everyone involved in the process or how "loved" the teacher is in the community, with the parents and with the students, removing a "bad" teacher could be a major hit to the sand in the administrator's political cup.

Many times, administrators throw in the towel saying, "It is not worth it," and they let the teacher stay. As a building-level principal, I witnessed times in which administrators were removed from their jobs for letting a teacher go. The truth was that the removal of the "bad" teacher took too much sand out of their political cup. I have witnessed biased accusations toward administrators who were accused of "having a hatchet" or of "cleaning house" for removing too many "bad" teachers.

If administrators get on the wrong side of removing a bad teacher, their political sand will run like water through their fingers. Every administrator, despite what they are being told when their contract is not renewed, knows the real reason—no more political sand. Removing bad teachers is not what they will be told was the reason why they were let go, but everyone sees the writing on the wall for that administrator after a "bad" teacher is terminated or allowed to resign. In too many observations there have been administrators so beaten down by the political games of the process that they themselves leave after a "bad" teacher is terminated or leaves.

The other political piece for administrators removing a bad teacher is the reality that, if you are a new administrator, it can be political suicide if you attempt to remove a teacher who has been in a school for many years. That teacher will produce years of wonderful, even glowing evaluations from previous administrators and the community will support that. The attempted removal will not end well for the administrator and every administrator knows that and backs away, and the "bad" teacher remains.

Again, all administrators are forced to make this painful decision at some point in their administrative careers. Shameful as it is to admit, it is true. I have witnessed this. What follows is the thought process.

Does one remove this teacher or begin the process to remove this teacher who one knows is bad based on their own personal observations, the data they have collected, and the results from that teacher's classroom at the cost of what one knows will be one's job down the road? That is a fact, folks. Any administrator who has removed a "bad" teacher, or worse, began the process to remove a bad teacher and lost that battle and the teacher was not removed, is one step closer to the door.

That decision will empty such an amount of political sand from their cup that they may not have the time or the ability to refill it. If that administrator loves their work, has a family, or needs that paycheck, then the decision to try to remove a "bad" teacher will be clouded by the question of, "is it worth it?" And the "bad" teacher remains.

As a side note here, teachers know this! "Bad" teachers are especially well-versed in the law, their contracts, and the steps necessary to remove them. It is almost an artistic cat-and-mouse game that they have become masterful at winning. Any administrator who continues with the mindset that they will always do "what is best for students regardless of what it costs them" is one day closer to leaving the very building they are protecting because doing so is political suicide.

As an administrator, some particulars become cardinal rules, but one in particular springs to mind. The tolerance level for "bad" teachers should be that if one would not want their own children in that teacher's classroom, then they should not want anyone's children to be in that teacher's classroom. That should be a baseline measurement.

That philosophy has been shared by me with countless other administrators who have not had their contracts renewed by school boards who thought they "were not a good fit," when everyone involved knew there was more to that story. Every administrator who has ever removed a "bad" teacher suffered a drain of sand from their political cup. How much sand? It depends. It depends on the process, the teacher, the support, the school board, the superintendent, the community, the students, the fallout, and the way in which the "bad" teacher left.

All in all, it is enough to say that getting rid of a "bad" teacher comes with a very high price. Sometimes, depending on the administrator and the teacher, too high of a price!

Curtain #18

The Spinning, Cracking, and Overwhelmed Teacher's Plates

Teachers' plates are full—no, overflowing—and we continue to put more and more on those plates and wonder why they are falling out of their hands.

There could be an entire book written about what we expect of our teachers today and how that target of expectation is moving and often shrouded in the clouds, open to the opinions and evaluations of whoever is in charge at the time.

When reflecting back on the expectations of first-year teachers years ago, and comparing those expectations to what is expected of teachers now, the workload has certainly more than tripled. Remember, from my vantage point more than half of the time that I spent in education was spent *in* the classroom, so clearly the sensitivity as to what was being asked of a teacher to do and the time that it takes to do it was forever in the forefront of my mind. I am and always was, due to my own experience as a teacher, hypersensitive to the demands I placed on teachers as an administrator.

Principals must be hyperconscious in regard to how much time teachers have to complete requests made of them. As a former teacher, I was aware that when adding anything "more" to teachers' already full plates, also required adding more time to their days. As state mandates changed, and as students' needs or data warranted, or as parents' demands increased, the time that teachers should be given typically does not exist.

This fear or super-consciousness, thoughtfulness, and consideration is not considered in every building and by every administrator. What is certain is that we continue to ask more and more of our teachers and give them less and less time to do it.

What is known is that many administrative colleagues (especially those who had not been in the classroom long), seldom have sympathy in regard to what they ask teachers to do, because they too felt their plates are full to overflowing and the work requirements "have to go somewhere." Common replies from administrative colleagues were that "Well the teachers are with the students all day" as an excuse to piling more work on them.

In today's classrooms we expect teachers to be counselors, nurses, therapists, policemen/women, detectives, lawyers, parents, friends, confidants, firemen/women, mechanics, seamstresses, actors/actresses, community servants, disciplinarians, moral compasses, custodians, shoppers, givers, artists, musicians, curriculum specialists, school safety specialists, curriculum directors, assessment managers, data analysts, active shooter trainers, secretaries, book keepers, data entry specialists, computer technicians, paper pushers, committee members, doctors, coaches, trainers, committee chair, contract negotiators, and, *when there is time*, teachers.

Every single year we expect more and more from our teachers yet continue, depending on the budget freezes, tax assessments, or political maneuverings at the state or higher level, to expect them to do it for less, or at best just pennies more than they did it in the previous year. The job description of a teacher is not the same as it was ten, heck even one, years ago.

We expect teachers to not only be able to manage the above list of jobs (and many, many more), but we expect them to do them perfectly, without any error. After all they are teachers, right? No teacher is allowed to ever make a grammatical mistake, how horrible. They are, after all, a teacher! No teacher is ever allowed to make a mathematical mistake, how inexcusable (even worse if they are a math teacher).

They are, after all, a teacher! No teacher is allowed to, at any given moment, spit out any useless trivia given to them by anyone and not know the answer. They are, after all, a teacher! No teacher is ever allowed to make any human mistake such as get divorced, get in an accident, have a child out of wedlock, or make any other immoral or unethical decision. They are, after all, a teacher!

Teachers are put on a platform which is almost impossible to consistently stay on without someone knocking them off. They are set to a standard, dated back long ago, that we cannot possibly expect them, if they are human, to maintain; yet, we continue to ask, no demand it. We state, as a society, that because these superhumans are "with children" every day, they must be perfect and completely without any error or flaw in any way, shape, or form.

And while they stand on that perch being pecked at, we, as a society, continue to put more and more on their plates; and we expect that, as good teachers, they must keep all of their plates spinning while remaining balanced on their perch. Good luck with that.

What is most difficult for teachers is that, far too often, actual teaching has become such a minimal part of their jobs. They are bombarded with so many committees, duties, meetings, and a myriad of other responsibilities in their day that preparing for their classroom, and actually teaching often gets put on a back burner in whatever time is left over. The constant needs of their students such as being fed, being comforted, being safe, and being loved, are often put so far in front of the faces of our teachers that teaching students the subject seems irrelevant.

Teachers must also move like puppets in coordination with the political maneuverings of Washington, DC, and local governments who push their political positions onto the backs of our teachers. Teachers must also endure listening to attacks from every news source that is utilizing their profession to gain political traction. Teachers know that the very thing they do every day, can and will be used against them at some point, yet they continue, despite the lack of much training, to do the best they can, every day, for the students they are trusted to serve.

So what is on our teacher's plates? Why are our teachers not teaching our students better? Why are our students not achieving at the level that governmental manipulators believe they should? The answer is actually quite simple. Every teacher and administrator knows it. What I am going to say will not shock educators, but it will, perhaps, shock those outside of education. Let me break down some of the bigger issues facing our teachers everyday, preventing them from doing what teachers do best—teach.

TEACHERS' DAYS ARE OVERSCHEDULED

It is not uncommon for a teacher to have little or no break in the day when they are not in front of students. Imagine that for a moment. Think about a work day that would give you no time to go to the bathroom, stand up and stretch, take a breather, walk away from an issue, regroup, talk to a co-worker, get a cup of coffee or a Coke to clear your head, or just breathe. That is true for too many teachers, especially elementary school teachers, each and every day.

If, as a teacher, they do not have time to run to the restroom can you imagine how they can possibly have time to look at how your students are achieving in that moment and re-adjust what they are teaching? Here is the fact. From the moment that teachers enter the building until the moment that they leave, they are responsible for children. They are with them, they are caring for them, they are teaching them, and they are monitoring them. They are constantly in charge of, or responsible for, children.

That seems like a no brainer. After all isn't that what they are supposed to be doing, teaching? Well, yes. But, in order to be a good teacher, teachers must be given time to evaluate data; plan engaging lessons; grade paperwork; make assessments; align curriculum with the standards; and plan fun, engaging, and meaningful work to deliver instructions.

Teaching, most would agree, does not happen spontaneously. Great teaching happens with thoughtful planning, data analyzing, curriculum planning, monitoring standards, creating careful assessments, differentiating instruction, and planning engaging lessons that inspire and teach those standards. When do teachers do that? When, while teachers are with students every moment, does this vital work of teaching happen? Not during the school day, that is certain.

Now, there must be an admission that most teachers do get about forty-five minutes during their day to do all that is listed above. Most teachers have a "prep period" during the day, every day. It varies from school to school, and the length of time is very different from elementary school to high school. It also depends on if the schedule has not been changed or delayed due to weather, so most of you reading this working outside of education would rebut this by saying, "I don't get a prep period in my job. That amount of time given every day should be enough for teachers to plan and prepare appropriately for their students."

During the "prep period" that teachers get, what must be accomplished is this: They often will have to attend some sort of meeting. They most likely will need to respond to multiple e-mails. They probably will have to return calls from parents. They may also need to prepare for observations or attend a meeting with an administrator after being observed. They need to copy materials for the next day's lessons. They need to check their mailbox and complete any forms that may need to be signed and returned. They need to schedule any necessary and upcoming parent conferences. Remember, depending on their student load, a teacher may have over one hundred "clients" whose families must be communicated with and updated.

They may need to attend a case conference or a requested parent conference. They need to make sure that whatever papers they have collected from their students have been and are getting graded in a timely manner so that parents can see them in a timely fashion. They need to update their lesson plans and perhaps revise them to be in compliance with the school's expectations and parents' needs. They need to complete whatever task is necessary to teach a great lesson, an amazing lab, or a neat lecture they are planning for the next day.

They need to quickly, very quickly, go to the bathroom and perhaps get a drink with enough caffeine to get them through the next few periods. They need to meet one on one with the student who is clearly having a rough day. They need to run next door and try to spend a few moments with the new teacher they promised to help. They need to complete so many other things that I could fill the remainder of this book listing, but let's assume you get my point. So what does happen?

We all know that no human being could possibly complete what has been listed (and the million things not listed) in one, single prep period a day. What do great teachers do? You already know the answer: They do all of their work after the students have gone home, during weekends, and during their breaks.

Think about your work schedule. You clock in and clock out. When you leave you are done. Not true for a teacher. They are home right now with their families waiting for them to all go to bed so they can plan tomorrow's lesson or grade your son or daughter's work before they come to school tomorrow. They are at school on the weekends and during their breaks trying to just "catch up."

There is no such thing as "done" for any teacher; if they are good, they are never, ever done. The stakes for learning have never been higher and teachers are feeling that pressure. They are also feeling the additional pressure, with no time, to even absorb the new requirements, let alone have time to put them in place. A room full of first graders is not going to sit quietly while their teacher researches another way to teach them that lesson since this one did not work.

No other career would allow this, yet we expect it of our teachers. If you were a boss today with employees that were expected to make a presentation on behalf of your company to a major investor, you would expect those employees to put in the time both on and off of the clock to prepare the best presentation to get you the investment. You would expect to see that group of employees working together in planning that presentation.

Not our teachers. At all times they are in front of children, so planning time is all *off the clock*. If you want to test this, take this challenge and drive by any school on a Saturday or Sunday, after school hours, or during school breaks; you will find a teacher's car in the parking lot. And, this is just the one who came to school; we can never account for the ones who are at home doing the same thing.

We have, as a society, expected our teachers to do whatever they need to teach our children, but have given them no time to do it. We have jam-packed their days too tightly and have given them no time to prepare but still expect them to "produce" amazing results. We shove the newest teaching methods down their throats during what little professional development time is provided, but allow them no time in their day to figure out how they will implement them into their lessons and their teaching.

There is no way that any human being could effectively complete what we ask our teachers to do on a day-to-day basis; yet we, as a society, continue to do it and we wonder why our system is broken.

TEACHERS ARE PROVIDED LITTLE OR NO TIME TO WORK COLLABORATIVELY, LEARN FROM OTHERS, RESEARCH BEST PRACTICES, AND GAIN NEW SKILLS

Though this has been referred to several times throughout this book, some of it bears repeating. Since every moment of teachers' time is spent with students, there is little, if any, time to learn and grow from each other or from outside resources regarding best practices. Some schools and teachers are lucky enough to still have professional development opportunities as a part of their day, week, or school year, and these teachers are at least getting some chance to learn and grow from colleagues, but far too many educators are left to fend for themselves. The time that they can work together collaboratively is done after school hours, on weekends, or on breaks at the expense of time with their families. This is a travesty and should not be permitted.

Do you remember having to get together in high school or college with a group of people with whom you had to complete a group project? It was sometimes difficult to get a group of high school students together on a Sunday afternoon to complete the project because you had to schedule around every one of the members' families. That was tough. It is no different for teachers. These are adults now with families and responsibilities of their own.

They are leaving those families and responsibilities, if they can, to meet at the school, after school, or on the weekends, or during a break, to do what should have been done during their school day. They are doing this off the clock, on their own time, and at the cost of their families. And that is for the teachers willing to make that sacrifice. Those teachers who cannot, or will not, are just not able to meet and are caught up as best as they can be. Is this any way to plan assessments, lessons, and classes for our students? This is what we, as a society, are expecting of our teachers.

We cannot continue to expect the very people who are teaching our children to not have the time in their days to adequately hone their craft. We would expect our doctor to go get additional training, and we understand if the office closes for a few days while he is out of town getting that training. We are relatively unbothered and not insulted when we have shown up to any other professional occupation and found out that the person who we were coming to see was out of the office attending a workshop. That does not bother us, and we simply reschedule our appointment.

Yet, wouldn't we be incensed if our teachers did that? For the life of me there is no way to understand why we, as a society, would allow the very people who teach in our schools to not have the proper training and to not be exposed to the latest research on a constant, ongoing basis. It leaves me scratching my head, because that is exactly what we do folks.

TEACHERS ARE EXPECTED TO RAISE OUR CHILDREN, SINCE MANY PARENTS ARE TOO BUSY TO DO SO

Parents, for a ton of different reasons, have continued to put more and more responsibilities on our schools. Parents' responsibilities will be addressed in a later chapter regarding our schools, but let's, for the sake of argument, make a list of the expectations placed on our schools and our teachers.

- Schools are expected to feed our children breakfast and lunch, and, depending on the socioeconomic status of the school, a snack should be fed to them as well. Plus, schools are to do that on a shoe-string budget and are expected to provide not only tasty meals that children would want to eat and not complain about, but to make them healthy, while also meeting state and federal guidelines. These standards are higher than the standards that most of us are using when deciding what to serve at our dinner tables tonight. Additionally, schools are to open their doors when not in session including for weather-related school closings so that they can continue to feed our children.
- Schools are expected to clothe our children. If a school requires a uniform, schools are expected to provide uniforms for those who cannot afford them. If schools are not requiring a school uniform they must constantly battle the parent and the student regarding what clothing is appropriate or inappropriate. They must also battle what clothing is in violation of the dress code or not in violation of the dress code.
- Schools are responsible for teaching moral issues, including sex education, to our children. Many schools now have, in addition to the curriculum taught in most health classes, actual sex education classes. These are held as early as fifth grade and continue to be taught year after year. Additionally, schools must teach a myriad of moral, social skills such as:

  How not to bully;
  How to protect yourself from a bully;
  How to be nice;
  How to share and what that looks like;
  How not to lie, and what will happen if you do lie;
  What stealing is, how to protect yourselves from thieves, and what will happen to you if you steal;
  How to be kind to one another;
  How to work collaboratively with others;
  How to listen and how to be heard;
  Winning and losing with dignity and grace;
  How to work hard for what you want in life;

How life can be, and is often, tough . . . but how you can rise above its challenges;
How words can be damaging and how to handle damaging words;
Self-esteem and how to be protect it;
Social media and all that it is and all that it can be.

This list could keep going and going, as, without question there is more, but here is the point: All of this has landed on the plates of our teachers who did not go to college for, or get a degree in these issues. Some, if they are parents themselves, feel more prepared to handle some of the moral and social issues as they come along, but others are simply not in a place in their lives where they can teach these skills themselves. That is not why they became a teacher in the first place.

They are being asked to do more and more with less and less to do it. Teachers are overwhelmed by the moral and social guidance required of them on a daily basis. That overwhelming pressure forces the disciplines/subjects, or what they were supposed to be teaching, to often get pushed to the back burner. And, as there continues to be a shortage of teachers, teachers must teach larger classes.

It is impossible to teach math to a hungry student. It is impossible, even insensitive, to teach science while a child is being bullied and is crying, yet we expect it of our teachers each and every day. Then we wonder why the curriculum, the very thing we send our children to school to learn, is being missed. Teachers are caught in the constant battle of "raising" the children in the classroom, while still finding time to teach the discipline/subject that they must teach.

They are constantly pulled, like a Stretch Armstrong doll, between doing what a child socially, mentally, or physically needs in the moment and teaching their subject. Teachers are emotionally distraught with the decision at any given moment between being the teacher who teaches the required subject and loving a child who does not need to learn material, but rather needs to feel love. This dichotomy is felt a hundred times a day by teachers, and they are constantly put in positions they did not leave college prepared for.

TEACHERS ARE HELD TO A HIGHER EXPECTATION THAN WE HOLD OURSELVES TO, AND WILL BE CRITICIZED OR ATTACKED FOR NOT DOING WHAT WE WOULD HAVE DONE . . . BUT DIDN'T

The expectations placed on our teachers continue to increase beyond teachers' capacities to meet those expectation. Each and every year we expect so much more from our teachers than we ever would expect from ourselves. We expect them to be perfect, without any flaw, yet no such person exists. We expect them to never make a mistake, yet no such perfect person exists either. We expect them, even without the right training and professional development, to teach any child right where they are and bring them up to the appropriate reading level or math level within one school year.

We expect our children (even when we, as parents, have moved our children each and every year to a different school system because we were "changing jobs") to make friends and be treated the same as all the other children though we know they are an entire school year behind. We expect teachers to teach their subjects at school and not ask parents to assist with the work at home after school; after all, that is not our job, it is the teachers' jobs. We expect our teachers to supply whatever materials they need to teach our children at their own cost . . . because that is their job. We expect for them to "deal" with whatever happens in their classroom regarding student behavior because, after all, we, as parents were not there, and they should be able to control their classrooms. Again, it is their job.

We, then, as a society, bully and attack our teachers but wonder why teachers are fleeing the classrooms at an exceedingly higher rate than they are entering the classrooms. We have become so self-righteous that we hold our teachers to a standard that too many, as parents, would never hold themselves to. There could be an entire book written about the attacks leveled at our teachers.

Turn on any news program—local or national—give it just a moment or two and you will see some news story attacking the work of our teachers and our schools. I will not spend any further time on this subject, but I will leave you with the following thought. It is difficult for teachers to "keep that smile" and come to work prepared to do what is in the best interest of the students, when their career is constantly under attack and is at the mercy of political maneuvering.

So, what is the solution to these plates spinning out of control? How do we balance what we are asking of our teachers? How do we help them keep their plates spinning without falling and still have the heart, the time, and the stamina to deal with a room full of active fourth graders or teach at the necessary rigor for the AP calculus exam? How can we do all that?

Below is a list. Many of the items on the list are commonsensical or logical, so much so that it will seem shocking that they are not already being implemented

For some, in education, this list will require a different way of thinking. It will also inconvenience others so that teachers can have what they need to teach. Here are just a few suggestions, from someone who has walked in teachers' shoes for twenty years, who has shared in their plight, who knows we can do better, and who wants so much more for the amazing men and women who are on the frontlines educating our students each and every day.

1. We, as a society, must decide what the defined role and expectation of a teacher is, and what role parents must play in education. Those lines have gotten blurrier and blurrier over the past several years and we must work together to focus them.
2. We cannot expect teachers, in the time that they have in a school day, to possibly address all of the "non-instructional" things we are putting on their plates. We must work as a collaborative team of parents, teachers, and administrators to focus on learning together and not fighting about the learning.
3. We must treat our teachers as the educational specialists that they are. We cannot continue to tie their days up with useless paperwork and bureaucracy, which keeps them from developing the very lessons that they need to prepare.
4. We need to provide teachers with support for some of the necessary tasks such as gathering supplies, printing materials, preparing labs, and preparing necessary materials for labs and lectures so that they can focus on preparing meaningful, engaging lessons to our students.
5. We must provide teachers with the necessary data warehouses and educational software to aid them in differentiating their lessons based on the data, Lexile reading and math scores, and level of learning for their students.
6. We must offer supports in classrooms where students' learning levels or disciplinary behaviors require more support and hands-on learning.
7. We must provide teachers time during their work day to grade, gather data, analyze data, plan meaningful lessons, collaborate, learn, and grow to be the teacher that students deserve.

Our teachers deserve this; our students must have this; and we, as a civilized society, must demand this if we ever want to see our schools change. We cannot continue to expect so much of our teachers and wonder why they cannot get the desired results necessary to help our schools. Teachers must be allowed to do the very thing we put them in the classrooms to do: teach. Teachers must have the time and the resources to plan lessons, create and evaluate assessments, and teach our children. We must make that our first priority.

Curtain #19

We Do Not Value Our Teachers

A book cannot be written about why our system is broken without addressing the issue of pay for our educators. It is a topic that will hit the hot button of many reading this book. It will hit the hot button because there has been such a disjointed connection between what teachers "do" as educators and what pay they "get" for doing it.

There has been, and until as a society we stop doing it there will always be, constant bantering back and forth regarding what our teachers make, their "vacations" that they have during school, how they are paid (taxes), and what we feel they are worth. Teaching has always been, because we all went to school and have that experience, the one career that everyone feels versed enough about to evaluate. Because we went to school ourselves, because we are sending our children to school, because we know where the school is, or have ever been in a school building, we feel as if we are experts on what a teacher's worth is, and therefore, how much they should be paid.

Let's begin with this analogy. Perhaps we can all agree that we, as a people, put value into the things we put our money toward. If something is important to us, we will invest in it. If it matters to us, we will purchase it. If we see stock in it, we will invest and put our monies toward it but we do not do that with our education system.

As a matter of fact, depending on the state, teachers' salaries are often tied to the taxes we pay on our homes, so we as stakeholders and homeowners feel some sense of entitlement as to what our teachers are being paid. We feel that since, in some states, our tax dollars will pay a teacher's salary, and we may not be making much money ourselves, then our teachers should not make any more. We truly believe that we have a right as taxpayers to dictate the salaries of our teachers and their raises. Let me give you a couple of examples.

A high school student has been overheard saying to a teacher, "Hey, since my mom and dad pay taxes and you are paid for by those taxes, you really work for me!" Without question this high school student did not devise that argument all on his or her own. I have been in the office with a parent who did not like something that a teacher did and have had them say to me, "Hey, I pay her salary. I should just fire her"; rest assured it is a common sentiment.

There has become such a sense of self-righteousness from so many parents and members of our communities that they really believe that if they are not pleased with one decision a teacher or an administrator makes, they have the right to dictate whether or not they remain employed and what their pay will be. These are just a few examples but believe this, *all* teachers have, at some point in their career, been accosted in the grocery store when someone finds out they are a teacher and heard, "Hey you kind of work for me. I mean you work in our schools, I live here, and I pay taxes, so I pay your salary."

Every teacher at some point will be picking up his or her car at the local mechanic and will hear the story of "blank" bad teacher who the community proudly "ran out of that school" because, after all, they paid her salary. It is simply ludicrous and is wildly out of hand. Our teachers clearly feel that attack on their very livelihoods . . . and their paychecks. There has become almost a sense of entitlement from us as a society that we should, and do, dictate what our teachers are worth.

And, with all of the recent attacks on education, the arguments about taxes and salaries, and the constant political power plays, our teachers are caught in that crossfire. Let me pause here, before some of you reading this say (because trust me every teacher has already heard it), "But teaching is a calling, how can that be measured in money?" Or, "There is no way that teachers can be paid what they are really worth, right?"

Or any teacher's favorite argument and one that they will hear within their first year of teaching from any of their nonteaching friends (because, trust me, any teacher with more than one year's experience would never think this), "Well, you don't work all summer long, and you have all these days off during the school year, so, you shouldn't make any more money." These are all true statements, but let me provide you with a few more facts.

Teachers are college-educated people with bachelors, master's, and doctorate degrees, who are not being paid at the rate of their nonteaching colleagues. It varies from state to state, but in many states, depending on the size of a teacher's family, their salary will put them close to the poverty range! We are allowing this to happen to our teachers. Then, for many young teachers, add in college debt and the idea of raising a family on a teacher's salary is one that causes them to leave the system.

There have been many studies that indicate that for many teachers, too many teachers, pay causes them to leave the profession, because they could not make ends meet and needed a higher paying job.

There is no way to track the number of teachers who come to their administrator's office with their resignation letters. These teachers were not leaving the building; they were leaving the profession. While sitting with them and being so saddened because they were great teachers and were making such an impact on students, came the realization in my heart that there was little question that they were right to leave.

As a former teacher who raised a family of five on a teacher's salary, the financial burden teaching creates hits home. There was a stark reality that, while, as a school system we would feel their loss, the mortgage company did not care what they did for a living and they had to take their degree and earn a better salary elsewhere.

This is sad enough to make one sick. The sadness is not for us personally and not even necessarily sadness for the school. The sadness is more for the profession—the idea that we have allowed ourselves to get to this point. The sadness is that we, as a society, have put so little value on our teachers that great teachers are flocking from our profession to make a respectable income to support their families. Sitting here, now, it is still unbelievable to me that we are allowing this as a society. We are allowing the people that instruct our children to be driven out of that field, because we do not value them enough to pay them a decent salary. Shame on us!

And here is a truth that every educator knows and every school system knows but will not discuss, and that is *experience* matters. Let me ask you this question before addressing experience of teachers. If you were an employer and you were given the opportunity to hire an employee with zero years of experience or one with ten years of experience, who would you hire? No brainer right?

Okay, one more question before exposing something that will blow your minds regarding experience, pay, and education. Imagine that you are an employer and you have the choice to hire an employee with *five* years of experience and an employee with *fifteen* years of experience. Again, who would you hire? So, what the desire is here is to make clear this shocking fact before going on. This is our dirty little secret that no one talks about. This is a pathetic fact that will leave those of you not in the educational world shocked!

In society we value experience, we pay for experienced employees, experience builds a résumé, experience gets higher pay; experience is valued, right? Many of you reading this are saying, that is such a stupid question. What is your point? Everyone who has a pulse knows that. Experience equals more money and most likely better jobs. In society, yes. In education, no!

You see, in education, as a teacher, you are punished for having more experience. Think about that statement for a moment. Experience in any other field in the world offers you mobility and better pay and better benefits. In education, experience traps you. It offers you no choices, no mobility, no opportunity to move and in many schools, experience places you at risk of losing your job, because you are at the top of the pay scale.

Have you ever wondered why teachers stay in a school district for so long and never move? According to the latest studies, students graduating from college will change jobs seventeen times in their lifetimes, but not teachers. Why you ask? Aren't schools seeking out the teachers with the *most experience*? Really, if a teacher does not like the pay from the school system they are at they move to another school system, right? Wrong. Here is truth that every school knows and no one talks about. Teachers have, depending on what they teach, only a small window of time to change or move schools.

When there is a teacher vacancy and a school needs to hire a teacher, most schools will look at, depending on the discipline and subject matter, the résumé of a teacher with under five years of experience. Five years (or so) of experience is the magic window of opportunity for teachers to move from one school district to another. Once a teacher has more than five years of experience, they become "too expensive." No one will hire them. No school will admit that to you, but it is without question a fact and every teacher knows it.

Now, a school district won't tell an applicant that their excess of experience is the reason they aren't getting interviewed or hired, because that would be age discrimination, now wouldn't it. But this is precisely what is happening. Remember, many years spent in the principal's chair made it clear to me that I was "not to even look at the application" if the applicant had more than five years of experience.

If I wanted to hire an applicant with more than five years of experience, I knew that I would have to prepare and pitch the "hard sell" as to the justification of why they were wanted or needed. Hard to wrap your brain around, isn't it? Nonteaching colleagues have heard it said for years that education is the only field in which we punish teachers for having too much experience. It is shocking! It seems impossible to wrap the brain around, but it is happening every day in our classrooms.

Here is an example. There are some disciplines that are "highly sought after" meaning that there are often more open teaching positions for them than there are teachers to fill them. Currently in this state that slot is high school math and science teachers. Because there is such a shortage of those teachers, the "five year rule" is out the window—mostly.

If there were an applicant who has less than five years experience in an area that is not highly sought after, regardless of what they teach, there must be a justification as to why they were not being hired, but, in the case of a highly sought after position, there was leeway given to look outside of that window. Now compare that with, for example, social studies teachers in this state. If a social studies position is posted in the state, there will be hundreds of applications in contrast to the three math or science applications received for any open position.

The first task, as a principal, would be to sort the pile of social studies teacher applicants separating out any teacher with more than five years of experience. The interview process would then begin with only the candidates *with less* than five years of experience. Yes, that is true.

The first criterion under consideration when hiring the social studies teacher was not who is the most experienced teacher to put in front of your child; it was who was the cheapest. Remember, again, that I'm not attacking first-year teachers; what is being said here is that when there are several openings the "best candidate" is not the first criterion that is considered. The first criterion is the cheapest, meaning the no-experience candidate.

Now, it goes without question that there will be some school districts reading this saying, "We look for the best candidate for the position," and that is true. Right now, after reading the above paragraph, there are some superintendents absolutely leaning back in their chairs when asked about this section of the book saying, "We here at 'insert any school district' search for the highest quality candidate for our students because we believe that that is most important for our students. Neither age nor experience are factors for our school district in looking for the best candidate for our students. . . ." Then ask them how many of the last twenty teachers that they have hired have less than five years of experience, and they will tell you they cannot provide that information as that is a "personnel issue."

The rest of the sentence is "with less than five years of experience" but they would never admit that. So, test me. Right now let me offer you a challenge. Go ask any administrator who has ever hired any teacher this question. "If you, as a building-level principal, have an open position in an area where there are several applicants, does how many years of experience that applicant has matter to you in your hiring practices?" Again, they will want to know why you are asking and if they can trust you, but this is a promise, the answer will be a yes.

They will probably laugh at you and wonder why you are asking such a stupid and obvious question. Or try this one: ask any teacher who has more than ten years of experience in an area that would have many applicants, "Would you be hired by any other school district with your years of experience?" Or, ask them this: "With your years of experience what is the likelihood of any other school district hiring you or any of your colleagues with that amount of experience?"

I can confidently say that if you ask that same question to teachers, they will laugh at you. Teachers are forced, because they know about the experience factor and their ability to change schools, to evaluate quickly in their teaching careers if the school system that they are at is a good fit for them. They learn as young teachers that they have a small window of opportunity to get out and change schools. They learn that they must decide within the first three to five years if they can spend the remaining twenty-five to thirty years of their career at this school.

Remember, it will not matter who the principal or the superintendent becomes; it will not matter who the new teachers that they will work with will be; it does not matter if the school changes a policy later that they do not like; it does not matter if they move and the school is now far from where they live; it does not matter if they are forced to change disciplines to one that they do not want to teach—none of that will matter. They know that they have a very small window in which to change schools and they will only be allowed that *one* change, so they must decide fast, decide once, and understand that that is it.

So, why should we care? Really, who cares if teachers cannot move from one school district to another if they have too much experience? Why should I, as a parent, care? Let's reframe the question. Do you care whether the best candidate teaches your son English or the least expensive candidate? Do you care that the teacher who is teaching your child to read (remember, your child will get one shot at learning how to read) is the most effective or the most cost effective? Do you care that there might be a teacher who wants to be in a different district because his or her life has changed and they feel trapped here?

Do you care that the teacher that is teaching your child is now driving forty-five minutes to work because her husband has changed jobs and they had to move so she can no longer stay after school to help your child because she has to get her own child from daycare before they close, and with the drive, she must leave school as soon as the students do? Do you care that the teacher in front of your child is miserable with the new administrators and is in constant arguments with them but knows she cannot leave? Does it matter to you that your daughter's teacher does not want to be teaching in this school district anymore, wants to leave, and knows they are too experienced to do so? Do you care? Now, does it matter? If it is your son or daughter in that room do you want that?

Okay, now hold your horses here for any new teacher that is about to rip this book apart saying, "I am a good teacher, and I have no experience. How dare you imply that just because I have less than five years of teaching, I am not a good teacher?" That is not what was said. Yes, you might be and that is not what the point is at all.

There are many young, first year, out-of-college rock stars who could teach circles around their far more experienced counterparts, but that is not the point. The point being made here is that what should be the most important criterion in hiring the person who is going to teach our children should be who is the best candidate, regardless of their years of experience. That criterion, more than any other, should dictate if a teacher is hired. Cutting teachers out of the interview process, and possibly our schools, due to their experience simply makes no sense.

Another analogy. Let's say your school has three first-grade teachers. During the summer all three leave—two retire and one leaves. Imagine where the first-grade team just went in ability to teach to first graders. This principal and this school district, just went from two very experienced teachers who really worked with a younger teacher to hiring a team of three brand new teachers. Remember hiring more experienced teachers to replace the ones that were lost is not an option.

Every teacher knows that old expression that "for every veteran teacher at the top of the pay scale, the district can hire two new teachers to replace them." So, what the district sees is a huge savings. There is no anger toward the school district and we all certainly understand, in these cost saving times, why schools are doing it, but it is our children who are paying the price. So, instead of exposing our first graders to over seventy-plus years of educational experience, these new first graders will now be exposed to zero years of experiences.

And, remember this is first grade! But, it would not matter what grade it was if it were your child, right? The same analogy could be used for any subject, any grade, and any school. Shouldn't we, for our children, be looking at the best candidates that fit the school, regardless of the years of experience?

In summation, what we are doing is offering the very people in front of our children as little money as possible compared to their college-educated and degreed counterparts, and if that is not bad enough, we are, depending on what they teach, trapping them in the same school system for their entire career. We are forcing twenty-somethings who have just begun a career to work more than one job to just stay afloat and pay their school loans and decide at this moment in their lives to pin themselves down to a school district or, depending on what they teach, be forced out of the career if they want to leave.

Who does that? And how can we do that to our teachers? We, as a society, must demand better of the very people who run our schools, change our children's lives, make such a huge impact on all of us; our teachers deserve better.

Curtain #20

Testing Was Pure at the Heart

Students in every grade level are measured, evaluated, and analyzed by a myriad of tests. Teaching has become focused on, measured by, and directed to tests in each and every grade level. We have focused our energies, our resources, and all direction to the measurement of tests in our schools so much so that we have lost sight of what we were attempting to measure in the first place.

Ah, testing. Testing has become the newest hot button in education. What to test, who to test, the length of the test, and the score of what the test measures have become so political that our children and our schools are caught in the crossfire. We have become so confused by fighting over the test, its value, and measurement that we have lost sight of the purpose of the test to begin with. There is so much political wrangling that we, as a society, have really lost sight of such simple concepts that are vital to educators when they plan their own evaluations and tests.

Politicians are so busy yelling "our schools are failing our kids" from the pulpit that they have lost sight of what true success is. There is so much arguing on both sides that no one is moving and no one is budging and we are in, what my father used to call, a good, old-fashioned "pissin' contest" that no one wins. We have become so focused on being right, by "knowing what is best for our students," by committing to tests (regardless of how stupid they are) just for the sake of being right, that our students are left like balls in an arcade game being bounced back and forth with little regard to where they land. We are so buried in the trees that we don't even know where the forest is anymore. We are just too busy fighting.

Caught in this crossfire are the sons and daughters of all of us. No one is asking the very people who know how to assist in this issue—the educators. No one is considering that perhaps we should invite to the table the very people who know their material and their standards the best. No educator would enter or prepare any form of assessment for their students without a very clear direction as to the three simple questions listed below. This is the curtain that should outrage you as a parent.

No educator is clear on any of the vital questions that are listed below. They might know one or two of them, or think they do, only to realize later they are sadly mistaken. Educators are held behind the curtain of state testing, and like players in a shell game, are left to "guess" what test will appear out of what shell and pray they have prepared their students appropriately. Educators are caught in a tornado of information that they "hear" about the test, and are left grabbing at the debris swirling around and hoping for the best. They know the tornado is coming.

They have read the reports, they know to brace, but they have no idea how big the storm is, if it will hit them, how they should brace for it, and what the fallout of that storm will do to both the students and to them. Is that how we run our schools? And, why, you ask is that happening? This curtain, friends, will, unfortunately, make you sick. So, grab a bag, something to wash your mouth out with, a cool washrag, and read on.

The real issues regarding the state tests are the lack of clarity with three very simple concepts:

- *What* material is on the test, *who* decides what is on the text, and *how* is that information communicated to all stakeholders?
- *What* is the goal of the test, *how* will it be measured, and *what* qualifies as success?
- *Who* should be tested, for *how long*, and *when*?

Let's start at the beginning, and in the next few chapters see if the muddy waters that have now become the testing scenario can be cleared without making you too sick. Let me begin by saying that it is rather doubtful that any educator will argue against the necessity of state testing. Almost every educator would argue that we, as a state and as a society, must have some barometer to measure success for all students in every classroom and in every state for every educator. Few educators would disagree to being held accountable to state tests as long as there were commonalities that we knew and agreed upon (that will be addressed in a later chapter).

No educator would disagree with an assessment to measure student learning and the need to measure what their students have learned. No good educator would be against knowing how the learning of the students in their classroom compares to the learning of like students in other grades and classes mirroring what they teach. No parent would be upset knowing that their child's learning is being measured and compared not only to their progression in their learning, but in how their child's learning compares to the state and local averages of learning for other children in the same grade or class.

These are what politicians would have you believe are the "issues" with the state tests, and while a few educators might support that argument, the vast majority in education do not. Political agendas would have you, as a society, believe that teachers are so mad about testing our students that they do not want the test at all. That is simply a half-truth being told to skew the issue and cloud the real problems with state testing, so, on behalf of every educator, hear this:

Tests do not scare us. We, as educators, are not frightened of assessing our students; we created assessments. We, as educators, are not in disagreement about the need to assess, so please stop making this about the idea of whether to assess students at all. That has never been nor will it ever be the argument from any educator. We, as educators, have been assessing our students since the day we walked into our classrooms.

We have measured learning, since we knew what measurements were, comparing the learning of our students to previous years and with other students. We, as educators, have taken tests as students from kindergarten to college and everywhere in between. We know the value of assessing knowledge and most educators are at complete peace with the concept of requiring a state exam to measure the learning of our students. That is not the issue, nor is it the worry for almost every educator teaching in classrooms today. That is what the media will tell you all the arguing is about, but let me tell you that having an assessment is *not* the issue.

For educators, the idea of the need to have a state assessment has never been a concern. While there are differing opinions regarding the length and the frequency of the test, few educators will argue that students and teachers should not be assessed. That is such a ridiculous argument that it is simply, regardless of what you are being told, not true.

So, let's agree to this point, for the sake of argument, and so that this curtain can be pulled back on the real issues regarding state testing. Educators are not arguing about whether or not there should be a state test to measure their students' learning. Now, that may have popped your bubble and you have found yourself saying, "I am so confused; I thought teachers were mad that there was even a state test at all measuring their students learning."

After all, "that is what I read in the paper; that is what I have heard on the news; that was what I was told. I have always heard that teachers are mad because they have to give a state assessment to their students at all." Well, if that is what you have "heard" and that is what you "believe" then hang on. Read on, and let me help you understand what really is behind the curtain and is not being discussed regarding state testing.

Very few in or out of education would disagree that the idea behind testing began as a pure metric. The idea began with the intention to ensure that every student, regardless of what school they went to, regardless of the poverty level of the school, regardless of the state, regardless of the socioeconomic makeup of the school, regardless of the location of the school, regardless of who the teachers and administrators were at the school, should be held to a minimum standard.

Every student, in whatever grade was being tested, should share the same base knowledge and know the same material regardless of where they were registered in school. Every student in every classroom across every state should be held to a minimum standard. That we all agree upon, measure, and assess. Agreed. Noble concept indeed. Seems so logical right?

Really, who would disagree with that? No one. No educator would disagree with what was just typed. No educator, parent, administrator, or stakeholder would disagree with the expectation that students in various grade levels, especially high school, should graduate with a minimum measured standard of knowledge. No one in their right mind, especially not any educator, would disagree that everyone should be held to the same standard and that standard should be assessed and measured with the same test and expectation. That is a no brainer comment, and most of you reading this are wondering if there has been some sort of brain loss to even make that a necessary point. Ah, if it were just that simple.

Curtain #21

The What, the Who, and the How of State Assessments

What material is on the state assessments, and who decides what is on the test, and how that information gets communicated to all stakeholders is a hide and seek, I know more than you know, game that is being played at the expense of our students. There is such a lack of clarity regarding the state tests that all schools are left with is a guessing game, at their students', and perhaps their own, expense.

Let me set the stage for this chapter by saying this: every teacher, no matter how long they have been teaching, utilizes a clear and concise manner to write, deliver, and prepare assessments. Most effective educators begin with the assessment in mind and teach backward to ensure that all material that will be taught aligns with the state standards and is assessed. Every teacher knows how to create effective assessments and many have been creating assessments that are aligned to state standards for years.

The manner that every educator, whether they have been teaching for one year or for twenty-one years, uses to establish and create any assessment is to follow these clear and simple steps:

1. Beginning with the state standards for that assessment, what is supposed to have been taught and therefore needs to be measured?
2. Align the state standards to the assessment to ensure that all standards that have been taught are being equally assessed.
3. Differentiate the test to ensure all levels of Bloom's taxonomy are being assessed. From the lowest of recall questions to the highest of synthesizing material that has been learned ensure that students not only know the material, but can demonstrate true application of the material.

4. Collaborate with previous grade levels for content clarity and with any other teacher teaching the same class or grade to ensure that all students in that grade or class are assessed the same. Usually, hopefully, there is professional development time for this . . . ah, but usually this is done on the teacher's own time (refer to chapter 12).

The four items listed above will be addressed in this chapter and the subsequent three items are in the chapters that follow.

5. Evaluate the testing time ensuring that the test will fit into one hour or less. May use more days if necessary for larger exams (semester) but not for daily, smaller, assessments. Consider your audience (the age of the students you are testing) for appropriate length of the test.
6. Determine how the assessment will be scored and measured (points per questions, points per standard, writing rubrics, and other grading rubrics). Ensure that each standard is being measured fairly and evenly throughout the assessment.
7. Determine when the test will be given and how that testing information will be communicated to students and parents so that everyone can prepare appropriately.

All educators have gone through this process each and every time they prepare an assessment for the children they educate; it is as normal to teachers as breathing. This does not cause them anxiety, and they are ready, willing, and able to complete the assessment knowing that these steps are vital to ensure that their assessment is measuring what they want and need to be measured.

Every effective educator that just read the above list read it and said, "Yes, that is how you create a meaningful and standard-aligned assessment." They are confident in this method, have been using it for years, and no one questions the validity of its tried and true success in preparing great assessments for students.

Remember, the above step-by-step process for preparing assessments is a reference to the normal semester exams, chapter tests, unit measurements, and daily assessments. It is not a reference to high-stakes tests. The process is common practice, even commonsense; every educator uses it to create, evaluate, and utilize assessments in their classrooms.

Remember too, that most of the tests that educators are preparing are not going to determine if the students passes or fails their class or grade. We can all agree that failing tests will be a detriment to students' success, GPA, and overall comprehension of their class, but failing one test will not, in most cases, cause students to fail a class.

It is a very different issue in regard to state assessments. In many states the state assessments are devised to determine if a student passes on to the next grade or graduates from high school at all. The "stakes" of one state assessment are so much greater than the longest, most difficult, high school semester exam that you can imagine. The stakes are so high that one test, for too many students, can make such a difference in their educational journey that it becomes a deal breaker for too many.

So let's slow down and really take a look at the clear steps listed above that are used to establish a great assessment. Let's take them apart one by one and do a little comparison, if you will, between the state assessments that are being pushed on our schools and the assessments being written by the professionals, the teachers, every day. Remember, what we are comparing here are the assessments given in our classrooms on a daily, weekly, monthly, yearly basis by our highly qualified teachers to those state tests that are dictated by each state to be given at a particular grade level or for a certain discipline (like algebra or English).

Most of us read those steps and, if you are not in the business of education, believe that the steps make sense, should be utilized in forming good assessments, and are clear and concise. Most would argue that it should seem logical that tests with such high stakes as our state test are going through the same rigorous standard to ensure our students' success. That would seem to make sense to most of us, right? Well, sorry to say, you would be wrong.

STEP ONE AND STEP TWO

Beginning with the state standards for that assessment, what is supposed to have been taught and therefore needs to be measured?

For any educator, starting with the state standards is relatively easy. Most educators have access to their state standards (though some are less accessible and are rather vague). Most schools and states have agreed on the state standards and are communicating those to their schools rather well. On the other hand there are states caught up in a political banter regarding what standards will be taught in what grade level and by whom. Let's, for arguments sake, rely on the standards that are clearly written, are easily accessible, and are measureable.

A state test is not so easy. You see, most state assessments are not written by educators. That may seem shocking, but as embarrassing as it is to say, that is true. They are also written by people who, aside from reading the standards on a paper, have had little to no experience teaching those standards. They have spent little or no time in a classroom interpreting those standards and therefore are left to their own interpretation of the standards or what they "believe the standards meant." Let me give you an analogy in order to make this point.

Imagine that we read the same book. Let's say the book we read was one of Shakespeare's plays. You have not read Shakespeare's plays since you were in high school a "few" years ago (no need to attack age). I, however, have taught Shakespeare for the past twenty years. Do you think, when looking at the standards regarding this great piece of literature, we would ask the same questions?

Do you think that we would have the same view of Shakespeare, or would approach questions to it in the same manner? Probably we would say not. Therein lies the point. Shouldn't the very people teaching the standards that are going to be assessed be involved in writing the very questions to assess them? Shouldn't the very people who are going to be held to standards and the assessments used to measure them be involved in the writing of the very tests they are going to be measured by? Does that not make so much sense that it is almost embarrassing to ask? It's so logical. But, that is simply not a reality for state tests. Well, maybe we will fare better in the next step.

STEP THREE

Differentiate the test to ensure all levels of Bloom's taxonomy are being assessed, from the lowest of recall questions to the highest of synthesizing material that has been learned, ensuring that students not only know the material but can demonstrate true application of the material.

This step is the most heated, right now. What level of questions should be asked and how many of those questions should be asked? What level of rigor should be utilized in the tests and at what level should that rigor be? Who decides that level of rigor? No educator would argue that pushing students to answer questions at a higher level of thinking is not vital. Pushing our students to think, analyze, synthesize, compare, contrast, solve, delve, evaluate, and measure their learning is vital and these are all necessary skills we must teach our students. That is not the point, nor is it even in the argument or issue here.

However, getting lost in the crossfire of the debate is the need to *know* the information before you can even get to the higher level of analyzing or comparing or solving the information. If a student does not know *what* an angle is, how can he or she be expected to compare it to other angles? If they have no idea *what* a noun is or how it is used in a sentence, how can they dare be expected to write a clear paragraph or a whole paper that can be understood by a reader? If a student has no idea where Indiana is in the United States, how can they begin to understand its global impact on goods and services? If students have never learned the periodic table, how can they possibly know what chemicals would react and cause an explosion in an experiment?

Again, there could be example after example but here is where the issue lies in regard to the level of questions in our state assessments. We have and are pushing our students to higher levels of engagement and assessing them at those higher levels so much that we are losing sight of the very knowledge it will take them to get there. Let's not get bogged down here on the debate of memorization versus the ability our students have to access knowledge at their fingertips.

The point here is this: If we, as educators, cannot agree on the level of questioning for our own tests and we are "in the business" how can someone writing a test that has probably never spent a day in the classroom possibly have that answer? If we cannot and do not agree on the frequency, the type, and the delivery of the types of questions we as educators believe should be asked on our state assessments, how can we expect those that know little about writing a test to know? Dare say, and based on the tests, they don't.

STEP FOUR

Collaborate with previous grade levels for content clarity and with any other teacher teaching the same class or grade to ensure that all students in that grade or class are assessed the same. Usually, hopefully, there is professional development time for this . . . ah, but usually this is done on the teacher's own time (refer to chapter 12).

This is a vital step that is happening in local schools. Teachers are staying after school and meeting with other teachers who teach the same discipline or teach the previous grade level to write, assess, and align their assessments. This is a common practice that is and has been happening in our schools for years: a group of teachers sitting around a table creating assessments based on previous grades or subjects designed to build on previous learning as well as measuring new learning. For educators this common practice is so normal, so at the core of writing good assessments, that it is just second nature and the way assessments are written.

This is not happening on the state level, for state tests. Teachers have no clue what is in the test. There has been little collaboration and sharing as to what they will need to ensure their students know going into those tests. Teachers are in the dark as to what is going to be emphasized, asked, delivered, and monitored on the test. They are left in the dark as to what they should be assisting their students in their classrooms with in order to ensure their success.

They are grasping at straws and hoping for the best because the very people who are supposed to help students prepare for the test have no idea what the test is about. Standards are unclear. And, teachers are in the dark as to the difficulty level and frequency of the types of questions that will be on the test.

For example, when I was a building-level principal, I had a meeting with our state department of education and fellow administrators. There were several of these meetings held throughout the state with the same agenda. Administrators were to select and attend one of these meetings in order to understand the new guidelines surrounding the current year's state testing.

The meeting was designed for building-level administrators to "clear up any confusion" regarding the year's state assessment. There had been a similar meeting held earlier that month for superintendents. Finally, there were also meetings held for teachers who taught the classes assessed by the state tests. I knew the confusion that accompanies state testing. A total of six other teachers were sent to two different meetings.

Additionally, there was another meeting held where the assistant principals (three of them) were sent to two other meetings. The superintendent also attended his own meeting for superintendents. So, be clear here, that is a total of ten educated adults attending *six* separate meetings to just be clear as to what was going to be assessed on the year's state test. Also, you need to take into account, at the time only high school students' tests were being addressed, so this meeting was focused only on secondary tests (in our state there were two of them); therefore, little attention was paid to any other information provided for any other tests other than the two that were within the "responsibility of this job."

When we all came back from the meetings (all ten of us), we had a meeting so we could share what we believed would be the focus of this year's test and how we could best prepare our students. At no point through this meeting and the several meetings we subsequently had did we ever agree on anything about the test. We were at the "same" meetings, or at least the "same" meeting based on the agenda provided, yet we, who are "in the business," walked away with sometimes diametrically opposing views of what we were to be assessing, and how it would be assessed and the types of questions that would be used.

There were so many points throughout this meeting and the following meetings that we either laughed at the ridiculousness of it or cried at our confusion and hurt for our students, or raged at the lack of clarity. You see, in our state, there were still fights as to what standards we would even assess, so at the time of our meetings we were unsure of the standards that were to be measured let alone how they would be measured and by what types of questions. Can you imagine that? What is being said here? Teachers are right now in front of classrooms preparing for a big state assessment and they have no idea of the following:

- What standards are being measured?

- By what types of questions?
- How often is each standard questioned? What emphasis should be place on that standard?
- When they will know the answers to any of these questions?

Yet, they, as teachers, have to walk into your child's classroom today and pretend that they know all of these answers, have their students take the test, and hope for the best. If you are a parent, that knowledge should send you in rage to your legislators, because, you see, based on the stakes these tests now hold, your child is being held hostage to them. Our children are being held captive to tests that the very people who are teaching them have little idea if they are appropriately preparing them for.

Our children are guinea pigs, if you will, to what the teachers and their schools "believe" are the requirements, the preparation, and the questions that your child will be held accountable for. On their behalf, teachers too are frustrated, embarrassed, upset, and at the mercy of what will be on the state test they are to give.

Which leads to the last issue of this chapter. The last issue regarding state tests for this chapter is in regard to how this information about the state tests is being communicated to the very stakeholders responsible for giving it. In any normal testing environment, teachers are rather clear in communicating the expectations of the assessment. Teachers provide students with study guides, sample questions, practice materials, practice assessments, and grading rubrics.

Rarely, in an effective educator's classroom, does any student go into an exam with *no* idea what is being assessed, how it is being assessed, and how it will be measured. Educators usually go one step further and communicate that information through Web sites, lesson plans, school data communication systems, newsletters, phone calls home, syllabi, and a myriad of other communication tools to make sure that both the parent and the student know the following:

- What will the test measure?
- How will it be measured?
- What weight will the test have on a student's grade/GPA?
- How long will the test be?
- When will the test take place?
- When will the grading be completed and grades posted for that assessment?
- Where can they contact and when if they have any questions, comments, or concerns?

Educators from kindergarten to high school are very aware that they must keep all stakeholders "in the loop" when it comes to communication of everything happening in their classrooms, but especially communication regarding assessments that carry such large weight and might adversely impact students' grades and ultimately their GPAs. All of that is a "no brainer" to any educator. Clarity surrounding assessments and the communication behind those assessments is a vital and expected piece of every effective educator's practice.

Yet, all of that is a mystery regarding state tests and communication. There is such a shroud of confusion, attack, finger pointing, and manipulation regarding state testing that no one seems to know what is going on at all. It is such a game that it often feels as though the right hand does not even know the left hand exists, let alone knows what it is doing. Educators have little knowledge as to what is on the state test, what it will measure, what weight it will carry based on each question, or when the results of the grading will be completed so they are unable to communicate that to the very people that matter the most—the students and their families.

Schools have been left to "guess" and to communicate their "best guess" to parents and students. They have been left feeling stupid, ill-equipped, unprepared, and downright angry that they do not and cannot provide the very information that is vital to the success of their students. They bear the brunt of the angry parent who wants to assist their student in preparing for the test, yet the educator knows they are offering only "their best guess" as to what is even going to be asked on the test and in what form of questioning.

Educators carry the outraged cry from a parent and a student who, after taking the state test for the past couple of years, has still not passed. Educators know in reality that the test the student failed the first time has changed each and every time they have taken it and, in reality, the educator does not know how the student should prepare or study for it, or how the student can be successful at it. Parents are less than pleased with the unfortunate shrug of the shoulder and sympathetic ear of the educator who frankly, has no answer to give. It leaves the school looking stupid, the parent frustrated at the system, and a child, lost.

So, with certainty you have read or heard in news stories, this has left some schools, educators, and parents desperate. Desperate times, for some, call for desperate measures—cheating. There has been a rash of leaked tests, hidden rubrics, political cheating, and outright lying to try to clear the fog of state testing. Make no mistake, there is no excuse for such despicable behavior. Lying and cheating under any guise is not acceptable, nor should it be tolerated.

The point that is being made here is this: When people feel pushed they sometimes react negatively. Sometimes, when people become wary of the attacks, feel the pressure of needing to pass, know the financial costs of failing, and have no idea of what they are really doing, they resort to extreme measures. Again, make no mistake, I am not excusing such behavior. This is simply a statement to assist you in understanding it.

All of this is so unnecessary and could be cleared up so easily if we would just work together. It seems so simplistic, but it is not. It seems like such an elementary statement to say, "You all just need to learn to play nice with each other," but as embarrassing as it is to say that, it is the simplest answer. We must learn to utilize the state assessments for what they were designed—to measure students' learning. We must move away from state testing being a "gotcha" or a manner to attack schools and teachers. How you ask? Here is how. Remember this chapter focused on what the material is, who decides what it is, and how the nature of the test is communicated, right? So, here is the solution for all of it.

WHAT?

The solution here is clarity and transparency. Stop arguing, and decide what standard is going to be assessed. Stop all of the political wrangling about do we measure this or do we measure that or how many times or with what weight. Decide on the standards, communicate the standards, and assess those standards. Be clear and communicate transparently. Stop the arguing and put your energies into creating a meaningful test that is communicated to everyone.

Once you have stopped the arguing about what standard we are going to assess, make that standard clear and concise in a logically printed document that is shared with *all* stakeholders. This document should be available for print, on the Web page, in the newspaper, in all media, on every school Web site, and communicated to parents. This communication should be made available on the first day of school or even in the summer before the child begins the assessed grade or class to assist parents in ensuring that the child is prepared.

This transparency also allows parents to provide tutors over the summer if their child is deficient in the necessary standards required on the assessment. These standards should be so clear that they are not wordy (we, as educators love to use big words and make big documents), and reader friendly, so that every student, every teacher, and every parent knows what every student in every grade level or class is learning and will be learning for the entire year based upon real examples provided to them. There should never be a question or confusion regarding the standards. They are the foundation, and without them, everything else will crumble.

The powers that be should prepare pre-assessments for the test to ensure that all stakeholders not only know where they stand in regard to the assessment but also have a good feel for the type of questions that will be asked of them on the actual assessment itself. Provide educators with examples of the types of questions, the amount of each type of question that will be asked, and the weight each question will hold in the overall assessments. Provide this information, again, in a clear, concise manner that is communicated to all stakeholders including the students themselves.

No one is asking that schools be given the test itself, but in the vein of clarity and shared leadership, no school should be left to wonder what the test will look like or be like. No school should ever again wonder what kind of questions will be asked and how many of them there will be. That just cannot continue to happen.

Standardized test makers should provide clearly when the test will take place, how long it will be, when it will be assessed (including the rubric), who will be scoring the test, when the scores will be available, how the scores will be communicated, and what interventions will be available for any student who is not successful on the test. All of this communication needs to be clearly communicated before the school year begins so that calendars can be made, preparations can be done, and teachers can appropriately prepare their lessons and assessments to align with them.

Also, tests should be given at the end of the school year not in the spring when many states test. Students should not be tested in spring when there is still one quarter of the school year left for learning. If the test is to measure the learning for the entire school year then the entire school year should be assessed.

Once these decisions have been made and communicated to schools, there cannot be any changes made during that school year. Once the decisions are made for that school year, they must remain that way regardless of the political party in power, the elections that may occur, the changes of who is in power, or any other political maneuvering that may happen during that school year. We must agree to that. Our students and our teachers deserve at least that minor consideration.

WHO?

The board creating the test should be comprised of educators, parents, and legislators to look at the standards, create an assessment, and create a rubric for grading the test and they should make sure that the voices of all educators are heard and listened to in regard to that standard, the assessment, and how we are going to assess those standards. No educator should feel in the dark in regard to the process or the manner in which the test is being devised, what they will be expected to teach their students, and how students will be measured. This must be a collaborative, team, shared approach—all of us coming together to measure the learning of our students.

Now, let's pause here to say that, just as in the debate surrounding teacher evaluations, there are those teachers who believe that "we can't test our kids." There are some educators, sorry as it is to say, reading this chapter regarding state testing saying that we should not have a state assessment at all. Sorry to every educator who is thinking this. This educator will not get in that boat with you.

We must test our children and measure their learning. Teaching is not about what we, as educators, teach. It must about *what our students learn*. We, as educators, must stop our own arguing regarding "if there should be a test at all" and put our amazing energies into creating a fair assessment that really measures what we are asking of our students in their classes every day. We must drop the idea that assessing our students is not what should be happening in our schools. We cannot stand on the platform of hypocrisy when in our own classrooms we are utilizing assessments every day.

As educators, we cannot spend our energies arguing "how dare they test our students" when, we as educators, assess our students every day. That is just part of good teaching. How can we possibly continue onto the next lesson, chapter, or unit not knowing what our students have learned in the previous one? So, let me take the pause button off here after saying this. We must assess our students throughout the state (and really we should agree across the country but heck we are not there, yet). We have to agree that the second grader sitting in your classroom right now should be held to the same standard as every other second grader throughout the state. We owe that to our most important stakeholders—our students.

So, now that we have moved past the righteous indignation of testing our students at all, let's work together to create the best assessment for measuring their level of achievement. Remember, we are going to work transparently. No cheating, no hiding, no shell game, no hidden agendas for all of us. The goal here is to work together to create an assessment that aligns to standards, considers our audience/students, utilizes various levels of Bloom's taxonomy for its questioning, assesses with a rubric we all understand, and measures our students.

Together we are a brilliant group of individuals who care about our students and their learning. That is, after all, why most of us got into the business of education to start with. We, as educators, should stand tall and demonstrate that we are not scared of any assessment. We have been writing and taking assessments our whole lives. All that is missing here for the success of any state assessment is the transparency, the collaboration, the consensus, and the clarity in creating a tool to measure. Without question, if we worked together, got our own personal and political agendas out of the way, we would be unstoppable. Anyone would love to run this committee because our students deserve it.

HOW?

In the above paragraph the how has been addressed, but a couple of points must be reiterated. We must remove the secrecy of this test from our educators, our parents, and most importantly our students. The political game of "I-know-something-you-don't-know" is just ridiculous. The sheer frustration of our teachers regarding their lack of knowledge of what to teach to prepare their students for the test needs to be addressed. It is flat out embarrassing, outraging, insulting, and completely unnecessary. Nothing will get any educator fired up more than this point.

Some of you reading this are confused. You cannot for the life of you imagine that any of the things you have just read in regard to state testing can possibly be true. If you are not in education, you are praying that this is not true and is rather an attempt to make a point and cannot fathom a time when any educator did not know exactly everything they needed to know in regard to the state assessments. You are certain of that.

Well, you see here is the curtain in regard to state testing: Education has become a political platform to get elected. Stand in front of any audience as a politician and tout how you are "going to fix our failing schools" and you are hitting a hot button for getting elected. You can be guaranteed the votes of:

- Every voter with a "beef" with their child's school;
- Every voter who loves their child's school and values education;
- Every voter who believes there should be state assessments;
- Every voter who believes that there should not be state assessments;
- Every voter who has a child in school;
- Every voter who has ever had a child in school;
- Every voter who had a good experience in school;
- Every voter who did not have a good experience in school.

Now after reading that list you are saying this, "Now wait a minute. Isn't that about everyone?" Yes, that is exactly the point. Stand on any political platform and tout what you "are going to do for education," and you will guarantee yourself votes, and state testing is the newest topic, and, depending on where your state is in this argument, it is the biggest hot button issue for politicians to use. How we are going to fix our failing schools has become the newest platform. It is the newest hand raising, paper pushing, screaming, and political rant.

Test it. Do this. Go listen to any politician from those in the White House to those in your local government, and they will make these statements in regards to state testing: "We must hold every teacher in every classroom accountable for the learning taking place in the classroom, and that learning must be measured. We must expect our schools, even those in poorer or challenged districts to be held to what students in more affluent areas are learning and being measured. We must expect that our teachers teach and our students learn and we must utilize a state assessment to measure that learning." Sound familiar?

Look like something that you have read or heard before? So has every educator. Every politician has made those "claims" and will continue to utilize that smokescreen of making them until we all realize that those rants are being made at the expense of our children.

Here is the embarrassing fact of our system in regard to the how we communicate about state tests: Your child will be, depending on their grade or class, sitting through a test *this year* that you, your child's teacher, your child's administration, or your child has limited knowledge about. You, as a parent, have no idea what is on it. You have no idea what standards are being measured. Your child's teacher has no idea if they have really prepared them adequately and appropriately for that test. Your child is not sure they are ready and feel their teacher's apprehension regarding the test.

Your child's school is crossing its fingers, hoping for the best and preparing for the worst in regard to the test your child is going to take. Every school is preparing for the media backlash when those results hit the media and continue to chastise our schools for "not doing well on the tests." Can you believe this? So sorry to say, this is all true. It will vary from teacher to teacher, state to state, and classroom to classroom, but it exists. And, again, all that can be said is so sorry—and hope you don't get mad.

So, how do we fix the how? Easy, we stop political grandstanding, and we get clear as to what we expect; then, we communicate it often and clearly. Often reiterated is, "There is no such thing as too much communication." Another thing often heard is, "No one needs to know what they need to know until they need to know it." We must utilize these two simple concepts in including and communicating the test and how it will be used and measured to all stakeholders.

Over time, daily staff notes proved to be an effective means of communication between the principal and the staff. Sometimes information provided in those staff notes would be repeated several times, and yet some would still ask on the day of the pep session about the pep session schedule that had been on staff notes for a week. "Hey what is the schedule today?" That question is a reminder that no one needs to know what they need to know until they need to know it. It demonstrates the difference between people who like to know a week in advance and were pleased that the schedule was on staff notes early because they "needed to know" a week in advance, and the teacher asking me the morning of the pep session who did not "need to know" until that day. Neither of those different preferences in teachers should anger or frustrate a principal as doing staff notes every day kept that constant communication flowing. Repeated or not, needing to know whenever they needed to know, the point that is being made is that there is no such thing as too much communication.

The parallel to the state assessments is that we must create that same ongoing clarity regarding tests. We must create a clear, concise, one- or two-page document with the types of questions, the standards assessed, and the grading rubric. We need to ensure that these documents are readable and user friendly for all stakeholders. We need to then communicate them often and repeatedly.

Some will "need to know" years in advance. Some will "need to know" months in advance. And finally, others will "need to know" weeks or days in advance. With that knowledge, there will be a need to communicate that information in a myriad of ways to ensure that everyone, every stakeholder, is calmed and assured about the what so they can focus on what is most important, the learning.

There can be no limit to the amount of times that we communicate the standards to be assessed, the methodology of the test, examples of the questions, the grading rubric, and the timeline for the test. No one, from the politicians to the teachers in the classrooms, can receive too much communication. We need to develop such a transparency that when asked about the test, stakeholders begin to say, "We've got it."

No one, at any level of the school system including students' families, should feel like they do not know what is being assessed, how it is being assessed, when it will be assessed, and how it will be graded. It should become so much a part of what we do that communication is that natural. There should be no mystery shrouding it. There can be no hiding from it. There must be a shared sense of leadership with it.

What should become evident is that when it comes to communicating even the simplest thing, it must be communicated to death. Our parents are busy raising their children, going to work, being a parent, caring for others, and living their lives. Communication with parents must be extensive.

Let's assume there was going to be an important parent meeting. That information must be put on the Web site, there must be mass text messages (several of them) sent out, there must be call announcements (several of them) made, it must be placed on the daily announcements at school, it must be placed on the yearly calendar sent home at the start of the school year and updated and sent home monthly, and finally it must be mentioned and included in every written form of communication and newsletter sent home from every teacher as well as from the main office.

At our meetings, parents were asked to sign in and check a box indicating how they knew about the meeting. That information was continually analyzed as to how the information was getting to parents. At one of the parent meetings a parent was overheard saying out loud to another parent, "I could check all of these boxes. I swear if you did not know about tonight's meeting, you must be living under a rock."

There was nothing as wonderful as that comment, because there would still be someone who told me that they did not know about the meeting, but there was a confidence on knowing that communication through several avenues had been provided and that information could be proven to the parent "that did not know." That is not what our politicians could say regarding state assessments.

So, what is the point here? The point here is that we must work together to decide what is going to be communicated, when it will be communicated, who will communicate it, in what manner it will be communicated, and how often it will be communicated. We must remove the secrecy, the I-know-something-you-don't-know, gotcha attitude, if what we truly value is measuring students' learning and not "catching teachers doing something wrong" and "political maneuvering."

Curtain #22

More What and the How of State Assessments

We are so caught up in political grandstanding and digging in our heels that we have lost sight of what the point of state assessments was in the first place. What the goal of the test is, how we are going to measure it, and what score or grade indicates success has been lost in the shuffle.

The stakes for these state assessments have risen dramatically over the past couple of years. The pendulum has swung from the test having no bearing at all for the classroom teacher and students frankly not taking the test seriously, to now the test becoming one of the most important measures toward a teacher getting a raise or at worse, keeping their jobs. Let that idea resonate with you before you get all sanctimonious.

The stakes for the state tests have gone from something that we used to give once a year and, aside from getting the data, had little impact on schools or students to today when schools, their funding, their very essence, are at stake. Teachers' jobs are on the line. Students' graduation or promotions to the next grade level are in jeopardy, and all of this behind a veil of confusion, mistrust, and flat out fear.

There will be some who are very quick to say, "Well, we should fire teachers if their students do not pass the state assessment. After all, that means that they did not teach my child and therefore they should be let go. I would be let go if I did something wrong at my job." Remember that this "something" is a state test that your child's teacher, if you have read the previous chapter, may know very little about.

Teachers have heard this argument for decades. Teachers are worn down and beat up over state assessments and the "weight" that they have. They are tired of the arguing and frankly just want answers, because the arguments have gotten so political and consequently so confused. There are really two sides to this argument. Politicians would have you believe that teachers are completely against state assessments and are scared to be held accountable to the tests.

The political agenda would continue by touting that "bad" teachers are not teaching their students, which is why their students are failing in our schools. Teachers would counter that argument by saying that most, though not all, are not at all scared by the accountability of the test and being held to that form of measurement. They are angered that they do not know what the test is (see the previous chapter). And, more to that point, they do not know how it will be measured in regard to their pay.

Remember the steps that were mentioned in the previous chapter about how every teacher plans and creates their assessment? Here are more steps that are missing for state assessments.

STEP FIVE

Evaluate the testing time ensuring that the test will fit into one hour or less. May use more days if necessary for larger exams (semester) but not for daily, smaller, assessments. Consider your audience (the age of the children or students you are testing) for appropriate length of the test.

Please remember that, as mentioned in the previous chapters, these steps are "just what effective educators do" in regard to putting together and evaluating assessments that they use every day, every week, every month, every semester, and every year in their classrooms. This is as normal to any educator as breathing. They give it no more thought than you would give to tying your shoelaces. They are aware that each and every step has value, has merit, and is critical to truly assessing what their students have learned.

No logical third-grade teacher would ever create an assessment for their third-grade class and tell parents "I am going to give your third-grade child one test that will last for more than four hours and will decide if your child will be retained in third grade. Oh, and by the way, I am not really sure what is on the test or how it will be assessed." Imagine getting a letter like this from your child's third-grade teacher:

> Hello parents of ________________________,
>
> I am writing to tell you that I will be testing your child next Tuesday. Well, I think it will be Tuesday. Well, at least I am planning on Tuesday.
>
> The test will last about four hours. I hope it is over in four hours because I don't have the computer lab after that and we have to get to lunch. So, I hope they finish in the four hours I am allotting, because if they don't I will just mark their answers wrong. Because, I told you we have to get to lunch and the computer lab is tied up in the afternoon.

I wish I could tell you what was going to be on the test, but, I am not quite sure. I have attached the fifty-five page document with all of the third-grade reading standards so that you can review that with your child if you want to. Now, I don't really know how many questions I am going to ask, how many points they will be worth, what type of questions they will be, or what the cut score will be for passing. I will decide on that, well, later.

I will decide on that once I have seen all of the tests, decide how everyone has done, and make a determination from there as to who passes and who gets held back for third grade. I know that sounds a little harsh, but, hey, that is reality, right?

Okay, so one more thing. As I cannot let your child leave the testing lab once they have started you might want to limit the fluid input the night before. We all know how third graders can be. And, be careful what you feed them, too, remember we are all pinned together in one small computer lab . . . with no windows.

Finally, please don't call me to complain or to ask any questions. I really don't have any answer, and I really don't care about your complaining. I mean, I can tell you that I care about your complaining but in reality, I don't. Sorry, just being honest.

Anyways, happy testing.
Sincerely,
Said no third-grade teacher anywhere.

Can you imagine this coming home from your child's school and from your child's teacher? You would be outraged and scream for that teacher's head on a platter with a fork. And, you would be right to do so. Yet, this is reality, folks. These are the answers that no one knows and every educator would love to send you this letter venting their frustration, but, if they value their jobs, they will go to the workroom, vent, put a smile on their face, and return to class to "teach" the unknown.

They have to prepare for a test, but they do not know if it will have ten or one hundred questions. They do not know if it will contain essays, short answer questions, open-ended questions, or other types of questions. They cannot answer the questions from their parents and their students and they feel frustrated and stupid every time they are asked.

STEP SIX

Determine how the assessment will be scored and measured (points per questions, points per standard, writing rubrics, and other grading rubrics). Ensure that each standard is being measured fairly and evenly throughout the assessment.

Begin by asking the question that every effective educator asks before preparing any assessment.

- What do I want students to know?
- What are we placing value on?
- What is important to know for this grade level or class?
- What would be measured as having "successfully" mastered the grade level or class?

We must begin with a clear goal for the test for our students. Not a goal to attack our teachers or attack our schools or to provide a political platform to be reelected but a clear, concise, student-centered, knowledge-demonstrating, fairly accessed, and communicated goal. We must stop the posturing from both sides and come to the assessment table with the students faces and hearts in mind for every decision that we make.

We must agree that, while we will not agree on every standard and every question, we must get ourselves out of this political tug of war. We must look into the eyes of the children in schools and demand that they deserve more than this constant bickering and fighting about what question is an accurate depiction of the assessment. We must involve the very people teaching the grade levels and subjects in the content of the tests!

Every educator knows that they must, after each assessment, look at each question and determine how many students missed that question and why. Is it a bad question or poorly worded? Or, was the material clearly not taught well enough, so that their students did not grasp the material in a manner that they could articulate it on the assessment? Every effective educator knows that they must ensure that the question(s) on assessments align with the standards that they are teaching in a manner in which the students they are teaching understand. They must also ensure that questions on assessments are grade-level appropriate. Educators know that they must continually look over the assessment, especially if students were not successful, and evaluate why the assessment was good or bad.

This is not true of state assessments. When state assessments are created, politicians and test makers proudly say we expect "blank" percent of students to fail this test. Every educator has listened to some test maker or politician proudly tout how difficult this year's test will be and how many they anticipate will fail. What is being said is this: Everyone involved in the making of that state assessment knows that many will not pass. What? Are you kidding me? That cannot be true, right? Wrong.

Let me help you with this analogy. Imagine your boss said to you, "Look, I bought you this great machine to help you make the parts you need for your engine. Now, I knew when I bought this machine that 40 percent of the bolts that came out of the machine would be no good and you would have to throw them away, but hey, that will mean that 60 percent of your bolts will be good, right? Oh, and one more thing. I am going to tie your pay, your raise, and your employment status to the effectiveness you have in creating these bolts in a timely manner." Your boss continues to explain that despite the "fault" in the machine, you are to produce the same amount of bolts every evening. Are you okay with that? No. Now who would do that? Oh, that's right. Politicians.

You see, tests are created with politicians knowing and counting on students not being successful. The more that students are not successful the better and larger their political platform is on which to stand, be reelected, and move their political agenda forward. There are those reading this who are so "down on the government" that they will say, "Well, here is just another example of governmental bureaucracy." But, we cannot do that.

This is more than just political bureaucracy; these are our children. Your son and your neighbor's daughter are caught up in this political fighting. This is hurting kids. This testing and political posturing is ruining some students and their ability to be successful in school. Both teachers and administrators have seen students doing well in every one of their other classes and choke on this test due to the weight, lack of focus, and knowledge that they are one of that "blank" percentage determined to fail. So, here is the question, are you okay if that is your child?

Once we agree on the standards, the rest can be worked out together. The solution here is a rather simple one: Begin by surveying teachers throughout your state regarding the standards, their understanding of the standards, and how they are currently assessing those standards. Put a committee together that is made up of educators, politicians, parents, administrators, and, depending on the grade, students and determine a clear and concise rubric for grading each section of the state assessments. Ensure that all levels of learning are being equally represented and assessed. Look at overall values and determine a minimum cut score to deem passing.

Provide schools with plenty of pre-assessments long before that student ever takes that test so that they can adequately provide the supports needed for students who may be deficient. Offer financial resources to remediate students who are grade levels behind or who, based on their needs, may require additional supports.

This is not Newton's Law, this is just common sense. We owe the very students that we are testing and the teachers and schools that we are holding accountable for the results of these tests the minimum courtesy of knowing *what* the goal of the tests are, *how* they are going to be measured, and *what score or grade* qualifies as success on that test. That is the bare minimum. On the contrary, it is an embarrassment to share the following story with you, but the point of how ridiculous this has gotten must be made.

In my state there has been so much political bullying that teachers and students do not know if an entire section of the test will be on the test. Now, mull this over in your mind: The section in question was never even mentioned as being on the test until after the school year had already started, so no educator had any time to prepare over the summer for the new material.

Additionally, they have no idea about what types of questions, how many questions, or the content of those questions will be on the test. Recently, due to some political fighting, the section added at the start of the school year may be removed. This fighting has been going on in the press and at the state house for months. The state test is less than one week away and, as embarrassing as it is to say, there is no resolution.

Wrap your brain around that one. Teachers and students are preparing for a section on the test that they did not even know about until after the school year started. They have no idea how it will be assessed or to what extent, and at this moment do not know if, despite their preparations for it all year, it will be tested at all.

Imagine if your boss told you to prepare a huge presentation for a client. You are given some of the content but not all of it. You have no idea if your presentation is to last fifteen minutes or four hours. You have the equivalent of an entire school year to prepare for it while you do the million other things you must do every day. Oh, and a couple more zingers for you. You have no idea how you will be evaluated for your presentation, but know only that you will be evaluated.

And, depending on that evaluation of your presentation, you may or may not get your raise, and at worst, could lose your job. And, if that is not enough for you to want to murder your boss and hide the body, a week before your presentation you are told that it may be cut completely. Would any human being in their right mind stand for that? Of course not. Yet, our schools are forced to stand for it each and every year. And, the casualties? Our kids!

So, what do we do? We come together. We get focused on what the goal of the state assessment was in the first place. We move past the political minutia and laser in on what we intended to measure in the first place, students' learning. We then, once we have the clear goal of the assessment, fine tune how we are going to measure that assessment. We create, communicate, and stick to a rubric that everyone understands and is working toward. We finally create a clear cut score and communicate that to every stakeholder so that everyone who enters the test knows:

- What is being tested;
- How it is being measured;
- What score is necessary to "pass" or "achieve mastery."

Again, not high-level science here, folks. It is called collaboration and shared leadership. Together we can assist our students in knowing what is expected of them and how they, too, are accountable to learning. It also creates an environment that testing is not to be created to *hurt* anyone. Testing is and should be created, as it was always meant to be, for the intent of *measuring* growth and learning.

Curtain #23

We Test Students to Death

Who should be tested, for how long, and when has become the latest aspect of our state assessments being wrangled over. What started as a four-hour test, for most grades and classes, has evolved into nothing short of ludicrous amounts of times spent testing our children. Students are tested more than we test professionals to gain licenses and certificates.

Thirty-plus years ago, there were tests given to students in various grades. The tests were used as a barometer of student learning. Students still graduated and were passed onto the next grade regardless of how they did on that test. The test, in most states, was only in about two to four grade levels and lasted no more than four hours total per grade level. Fast forward to today.

Now students are being tested in many states in at least six grade levels and the test can take, per grade level, between nine and twelve hours. Additionally, in many grade levels, if a student does not pass that test, they cannot move on to the next grade level or graduate from high school. So, let you mind wrap around this for a moment. Your eight-year-old is taking a test, one test, to decide if they can move on to the next grade level.

And, your student in high school is taking a test to decide, despite their GPA and classes that they have taken and passed, if they can graduate from high school with a diploma. Not only that, your children are sitting in a test for more hours than your doctor sat in an exam to get his or her medical license to determine if they move on to the next grade.

Your attorney did not spend as long in a classroom testing to pass his or her state bar to practice law as your ten-year-old will spend taking the state test to decide if they will move on to the next grade level. If that sounds shocking to you, then let's not even measure the amount of time in class teachers and students are spending preparing to take that test, because if we totaled that amount of time, that information just might push us all over the edge.

We are so busy fighting about how long the test will be and who should be tested at all that it has caused mass confusion, frustration, and sheer anger on every side. Parents feel frustrated as they do not know how to assist their child; the schools do not have any answers to give in support, and the politicians are busy touting how the newest assessment will "measure student growth."

I will tell you another story shortly, but first, let's understand what goes into preparing students and any school building for state assessments. You will not believe me when you hear this, but first-hand experience can tell you that this is happening in every school across the United States.

When the state test occurs during the school year may vary from state to state, but be guaranteed that the meetings, the planning, and the items are happening in every building, every year. The first example is of the extreme planning necessary for one test in one state for one class, algebra, but could be from any state test and subject or grade level.

Preparation for the state assessment begins in the summer before school starts by:

- Evaluating last year's data.
- Looking at the released questions from last year's test to drive this year's curriculum, testing, pre-assessing, post-assessing, data modifications, and follow through.
- Place students who were not successful in some sort of remediation (some more than one depending on their scores). Balance that remediation with the other required courses to graduate from high school.
- Balance the master schedule to allow students every opportunity to be remediated, because, as every administrator knows, testing drives the master schedule.
- Look at testing times, based on the information you have now that you know will change, and where that will fit into the calendar.
- Cancel all major events around testing. Make sure athletics knows and does not schedule games before major testing dates.
- Attend all meetings held throughout the summer to discuss, outline, and learn about this year's state test.

Continues at the start of the school year:

- Meet with upset parents whose children have been placed in remediation classes again.

- Place new and incoming students into the necessary remediation classes as soon as you know their scores. (This can sometimes be four to six weeks after school has started.) Make that phone call to the unhappy parent and student whose schedule has changed.
- Check to see if the testing dates and times you learned over the summer are still the same (and they are usually not, if they were posted at all) and make the necessary modifications to the calendar.
- Work with staff to communicate the dates of testing so as to not have tests in their other classes and discourage major assignments being done while state testing is occurring.
- Work with your special education population to ensure that the proper supports are in place and are being constantly monitored and measured regarding students' progress and learning toward the test.
- Book/lock out the lab for the testing around Christmastime for students who did not pass last year.
- Make sure books are ordered, labels are accounted for, computers are uploaded, students and parents are aware.
- Communicate, communicate, and communicate with the students and their families the value and the importance of the test. Have parent meetings, put out newsletters, and work with families to assist them in their child being successful.

Keep going at the start of the second semester:

- Reevaluate and reschedule students that did pass at Christmas and those who did not. Remember this information, depending on the winter testing times, may not be made available until two to four weeks into the semester, so classes may need to be created or deleted uprooting a countless number of students' schedules to accommodate students' testing schedules.
- Work with staff to communicate the dates of testing so as to not have tests in their other classes while state testing is occurring and discourage major assignments being done.
- Work with your special education population to ensure that the proper supports are in place and are being constantly monitored and measured regarding students' progress and learning toward the test.
- Book/lock out the lab for the testing around testing time for students who need to test. Provide different labs and areas for special education students as they might have different needs, for those who have never taken the test before, and for those who are taking it again.
- Make sure books are ordered, labels are accounted for, computers are uploaded, students and parents are aware.

- Communicate, communicate, and communicate with the students and their families the value and the importance of the test. Have parent meetings, put out newsletters, and work with families to assist them in their child being successful.
- Create a schedule to accommodate all students who are testing while trying to continue learning for those who are not testing.
- Wait for the results, especially for the senior who needs this test to graduate and quickly make the modifications in his or her diploma as is necessary based on the results of the test.

Floored, aren't you? But throw in another monkey wrench. In this state this past spring, one week before the test, there was a political dance where no one knew how long the test would be. Imagine that. Not only can labs not be booked, schedules cannot be made, and students cannot be adequately prepared, but schools are also at the mercy of political fighting to even get a test going.

Teachers are ready to test, students are ready to take the test (or as ready as they can be), and politicians are too busy arguing about how long the test will be? It is like two children on the playground fighting over and pulling a toy from side to side except this is no toy . . . it is our children and our teachers who are the tug toys.

So how do we fix it? Again, the answer is easy. It is shameful to think that when a test is less than a week away any conversation is being held regarding that test aside from the fact that it is going to happen and when. The length of the test, and what grades and classes should be tested and when must be agreed upon and determined long before the school year ends. The summer, early on, is the time to communicate with all stakeholders the timeframe of the test and who will be tested. It is so easy, but we must get out of the way of each other's political standings and remember the very reason we created the test at all . . . to measure students' learning!

Curtain #24

A Parent Can Make or Break a School System

Parents are both the cornerstone of support and the catalyst of division for any school system. Have a parent's support and faith in your school and you are on crystal blue waters, sailing together to the promised land of wonderful education for children. Be in the crosshairs of a ruthless parent and your school is at the mercy of their whim while your boat, with all of your students in it, is tossed into a hurricane with no end in sight. It depends on the parents.

It does not matter if you have one child or twenty children, if you are a grandparent or the favorite aunt or uncle, you have had some sort of engagement with a school. You have attended a meeting, called a teacher, spoke to an administrator, volunteered in your child's class, mailed a letter, sent an e-mail, or communicated in one shape or another with a school. If you have air in your lungs, you have probably experienced a myriad of emotions toward the school.

If you have ever had a child in school for more than one year you have felt pride, you have experienced sadness, you have been happy, you have felt frustration, you have worried, you have been anxious, and you have cried. All of these emotions are normal and understandable to everyone in a school. Remember almost every person in your child's school is a parent themselves. They too have felt your joy, shared in your sadness, anticipated your anxiety, heard your frustration, shared your worry, and celebrated your happiness.

Let's be clear that as you read the following few chapters that the view from the parent's perspective is one that is shared by the author. Yes, though teaching was my career for twenty years and yes, administration was my job for another ten years, aside from being a wife, being a mom is my most important job.

As a parent, I have personally experienced each and every one of the emotions listed above. I completely understand them, I have a sense of living them, a knowledge in feeling them, and I know exactly what they are. Let me clarify to say that, as both a teacher and an administrator, there were countless opportunities to work with amazing parents who have been such a blessing to us. Sadly, not all parents share in that collaborative spirit and are *damaging our schools*.

Unfortunately, because of the behavior of a small, yet very vocal, group of parents our administrators and teachers are becoming more and more reactive, defensive, and frightened, too often. This small minority of parents are holding our schools hostage, and making them afraid to make decisions. Schools are becoming paralyzed in fear of repercussions brought about by some of these parents, rather than making decisions based on what is best for all of the children in their classrooms or schools.

These are the chapters that must be shared. This is a curtain that must be pulled aside, because most of us as parents have no idea how the small vocal minority are negatively impacting our schools. The curtain is simple, friends, and it is this: There is a small vocal minority of parents in each and every school from every elementary school to every high school, who, because of their self-serving, bullying tactics, are making schools scared to death to make any decisions that will go against them, despite whether that decision is what is right for our children or not.

In order for any relationship to be successful it must begin with trust. Principals must trust that the teachers are highly qualified and know how to teach, because it is impossible for the principal to be in every classroom every moment of the day. Teachers have to trust that the administration knows there is teaching happening in the classroom and supports it appropriately. Parents' trust has to be established by the school complying with a few things.

- The children's school must do everything in its power to keep children safe.
- The children's teachers should love, encourage, support, and educate the children to the best of their abilities.
- The children's school must understand the appropriate curriculum necessary to make them successful in each grade level that they were in.
- The children's school provides busses that were inspected and safe, and the employed drivers must get the children to and from school safely.
- The children's administrators must hire effective instructional leaders and support and push the children's teachers to provide the best instruction to children.

- The children's administration must be frugal and responsible with the monies provided them to hire the best teachers, to offer the best classes, and to support the buildings as much as possible.
- The children's teachers and administration must be well-versed in the latest state and federal requirements for state testing and remediation of the children if necessary.
- The children's teachers and administration must be well-versed in the latest state and federal requirements for graduation and post-secondary planning.
- The children's teachers and administration must provide proper supports for the fine arts, athletics, and any other social or emotional clubs or organizations that the children want or need to make them well-rounded students.
- The children's school has to hire appropriate staff to clean and maintain the buildings children are in and must ensure that those buildings are safe, in code, and inspected often.

The list could keep going and going but here is the point: There has to be a trust that those things are happening, because parents cannot ensure those things are being addressed on their own. After all, for most of us as parents, we have full-time jobs ourselves. We have families to raise, dinners to cook, and lives to live outside of the school that our children attend. Trust must be established that the very people in that building were "taking care of the education for our children."

The entire time that my children were going to school, I knew the "other side" of children's learning more than most of my children's friends' parents did. I understood the curriculum and state testing mandates and assisted my children's friends.

I had the ability to devise a high school, four-year plan for my children to graduate successfully and be admitted to a college or university, because that was something I did every day. After attending a parent meeting at my children's school I would hold a "meeting after the meeting" to break down the material we just learned, because I was familiar with the lingo and manner of the meetings. When our own children were completing their own four-year plans or their own classes I was able, always, to challenge any inaccuracies on their schedules or plans because, again, as for many educators my life was spent "in the business" of education.

For twenty-one years, our school never broke the trust central to a parent's concerns. For twenty-one years we had at least one child in one school building and at times in all three schools (elementary, junior high school, and high school), yet never at any point was there not trust between us and our children's school to do the right thing for our children.

Were there parent meetings with our children's teachers? Of course there were. Were there ever meetings held with administration in one of our children's schools? Of course. Was there ever a call or communication with a teacher questioning an assignment, or a test, or a grade? Of course. Was there ever an e-mail sent and a meeting scheduled to address questions or concerns? Again, of course there was. But, never, not after any meeting, not after any disagreement, not after any challenge, did we stop trusting the school to do what was in the best interest of the children. And, they always did.

Now before some of you reading this posture and start saying, "Well you just don't know my child's school. They are idiots and I will keep going up to that school any time I need to." Or to the person reading this yelling at the book saying, "Of course this lady is saying all of this. She was a principal and a teacher. She does not know my child's school." Let me say this to you: breathe, rest, and read on.

You are right, I do not claim to have personal knowledge regarding your child, and you are right, I do not claim to have been to every school in every state, but here is what I can say based on my experience. We must begin to trust each other and learn and grow and make mistakes together, free from attacks and a bullying type of mentality. In the upcoming chapters as parents and their role in breaking our system is examined, in no way, shape, or form is there an implication made that trust should be a blank ticket to schools.

What is being said here is to define trust as faith. Define trust as the knowledge that while the very people who are working with our children are humans, they care about the children they are blessed to educate. Because they are humans, they will, undoubtedly, make mistakes. Trust that together we can work to fix those mistakes and learn from them so as to not have them repeated. And trust that no matter what decision is made, that the people in our schools in and out of the classroom do and always will have our children's best interests at heart.

You see, lack of trust between parents and teachers and parents and administration is at the core of what is breaking the system in our schools. Because there is such a lack of trust and a "gotcha" kind of attitude among too many parents, schools and parents have become adversaries and not partners in their children's education. Children are feeling that division and are aware of that adversarial relationship, and it is destroying their relationship with their teachers, as well. So, what we end up with is a ton of finger pointing, accusations, and downright nastiness toward each other in which no one wins, and our children lose.

In the coming chapters, you will be given a "behind the scenes look" at what adversarial relationships between parents and schools are doing to our schools. This venomous viciousness is escalating and it is getting us nowhere. Schools have become so busy protecting themselves against attacks, that the root of the problem has become lost. Hopefully, the next few chapters about what is being allowed to happen in our schools will anger you so much that you, as parents, who trust your children's schools, revolt to the point that it stops.

Let's pause here and say this: Every school is blessed with what we, in education, call the "silent majority" of parents. Who are these "silent majority"? Let me tell you who they are, because they are God's gift to every educator and, before having to get dirty explaining "the other side," let me tell you who you are, but you probably already know.

- You are the parent who returns a teacher's call about their child and offers support, encouragement, and follow through regarding your child's learning or behavior in the classroom.
- You are the parent who knows your child's teacher by name, and reaches out to them often to "check up on your child."
- You are the parent who has sent that e-mail of thanks (that trust me your child's teacher still has) for no reason other than the fact that you just wanted to.
- You are the parent who, when there has been a concern with your child, set a meeting, came to the meeting on time, and came with a collaborative, supportive spirit to come to a resolution that would benefit your child.
- You are the parent who has baked cookies, donated for class parties, attended the PTO meeting, volunteered, and supported your child's school whenever and wherever you could.
- You are the parent who despite some unfortunate situations or personalities you may not have liked, have never trash talked your child's school or teachers to anyone, especially not to your children.
- You are the parent who expects that your child comes to school, on time, every day and respects their teachers, behaves, does their work, and learns.
- You are the parent who would come to the school in a minute if your child's behavior was inappropriate or out of line, and your child shudders in fear knowing you would do so.
- You have never thought of your child's school as a babysitter while you have to work, and therefore, are not upset at school closures or days off of school for staff professional development.
- You are the parent who would never just show up to your child's teacher or principal demanding to see them because you understand that your child is not the only child in the school.
- You are the parent who ensures that your child is at school every day and does everything to avoid them missing school for routine medical and dental appointments.
- You are the parent who would never consider pulling your child out of school to take them shopping, visit someone, take a vacation, or whatever

other reason you could name because you value your child's education and their need to be in school.
- You are the parent who, if your child would get called to the office, would support the school, discipline your child, and expect that the behavior would not happen again.
- You are the parent that respects the security "hoops" you now must jump through just to enter the building including your signing in and signing out because you understand that those same security measures are keeping your child safe.
- You respect your child's school, its teachers, and the administration and are grateful for what they do, have done, and continue to do every day to prepare your child for their next step on their educational journey.

You are *not* who is going to be addressed in the following chapters. But, we must address the vocal few who are making schools change and are driving decisions that are affecting your children.

Educators cannot tell you that the changes are being made, but they are. Educators cannot tell you, because they know the power of these vocal few, and they do not want to be on their bad side. Educators cannot tell you that some of these vocal few flat out frighten them and have threatened their person or their job. Educators will not tell you the names that these vocal few have called them, the threatening e-mails they have sent them, and the berating they have felt from them.

And, most importantly, any administrator will not tell you how the vocal few use the media as their bullet of choice to up the ante on their tactics. Schools will not tell you that, due to fear, they far too often give in to this vocal minority to avoid upsetting them at almost any cost. But, here comes this curtain. This is the curtain, of the very vocal few, that is setting the stage of education for all of our children.

Curtain #25

Discipline at Schools Has Gotten Out of Hand

Discipline has become the hot button that every school knows can blow up their world. Whether or not a student is disciplined, how they are disciplined, how frequently they are disciplined, and how severely a student is disciplined can change the dynamics of a school, the teacher, and the administrator involved. Parents' reactions of support or disagreement are the barometer for what will happen next to the school.

Can we all agree that discipline is vital to the success of our schools? Seems like such a silly question, right? It seems silly to think that there would be anyone who would question that schools must have a discipline policy, it must be followed, and every student, regardless of who they are, should be held to the same policy. That is all very logical, and most would agree with you that that statement makes so much sense.

Unfortunately, that is not happening in our schools. Discipline and support of that discipline from parents can have large, even dangerous overtones for a school. Having a parent disagree can threaten the employment of those making the decision or in worse cases threaten the safety of the school building as a whole.

Before going any further let's establish some commonalities that we must be working from. Think of the word discipline in your household with your own children for a moment. How you parent your children may be exactly how you were parented based on your upbringing. You have probably been in a restaurant or at the local grocery store and saw a child being disciplined and thought that the discipline was either too harsh or not harsh enough. You had an opinion.

You have been out with friends and their children when their child began misbehaving, and you watched the discipline that was given to that child. Whether you thought the discipline levied was appropriate or way out of line, you had an opinion. You have been at church when babies begin crying; some parents take their children out of church, while others stay in church and attempt to console their crying children.

Whether the parent took the child out or the other parent kept their crying child in church, you had an opinion as to which made the proper choice. You have had conversations with your friends, who believe that children should not be disciplined at all and should "discover how to behave," while you adopt a "spare the rod and spoil the child" philosophy.

In schools we have classrooms full of children, some of whom have been allowed to cry in church and others that were taken out; some "discovered how to behave" and were "spared the rod," while others may have been disciplined too harshly; some have been disciplined in a manner that might be thought of as out of line and others been disciplined by what some would view as not strict enough.

A teacher and a school as a whole must discipline their "house" remembering that they are not "raising" students, but rather creating an environment for everyone in the building to be able to learn and to teach. Turn on any news story, however, or read any parenting magazine and you will soon discover that discipline, what it looks like, and how it is manifested is a heated topic that leaves schools on the constant defensive.

You see, schools operate with the law of *in loco parentis*. *In loco parentis* is a Latin term meaning "instead of a parent" or "in place of a parent." In other words, the moment a child enters a school building, the school assumes *in loco parentis*. Since a school is responsible for every student in the building, including yours, they must develop a discipline policy that protects and promotes education of the majority, regardless of whether or not it may line up with a parent's personal discipline pedagogy and methodology, and therein begins the tug of war.

Parents, especially untrusting parents, are not too keen on giving away any decision regarding their child, especially in regard to discipline. Yet, that control must be rescinded for the sake of the whole, rather than the one. Do you know any parents who have five hundred to four thousand children? That's the size of any given school. So, for the sake of argument, we have to move forward understanding that schools have the legal right and the legal support to make disciplinary decisions, and they must look at the good of the whole rather than the desires of a few.

Okay, so the majority of you reading this part about discipline are saying, "Got it." Schools have children coming to them with many different upbringings and discipline beliefs, and schools have more than just one child to discipline, and they have to look at the big picture to do what is best for everyone, even if it is not what a parent may like or would have done themselves . . . got it! What is your point?

The point here is that the vocal few would disagree with you. The vocal few would tell you that a school must mirror the manner in which they discipline their child. The vocal few will tell you that they do not care who or how many other students are in the school or who was affected by the disciplinary choice of their child. Their child should not be disciplined. The vocal few will tell you that if you, as a school, have the audacity to discipline their child, they will go to every news media outlet both written or on air and "destroy" the school.

And, for the very scary situations, they may return to your building with intentions to do bodily harm to you, the teacher, or any other adult involved in the discipline of their child. Sound unreal? Sound like a fish tale? Sound like it could not happen in your child's school? Think again. Let me tell you just a couple of personal stories and give you the "types" of vocal few that are being described and are involved in every school across this nation. Clearly the stories have been changed to hide and protect those involved but . . . well, you will see what is meant.

STORY #1: BUT MY CHILD DID NOT DO IT . . .

In a small school's seventh grade classroom, Johnny was caught looking off of the paper of Suzie in front of him. Mrs. M saw it and Suzie admits that she tried to cover her paper but she believes that Johnny was indeed looking at it. After class Mrs. M confronts Johnny, who vehemently disagrees that he was doing anything. He did not look at her paper and chastises Suzie for being a liar for even saying it.

Even when Mrs. M tells Johnny that she indeed saw him do it, he continues to say, "Well, I don't know what you thought you saw but I was not looking at anyone's paper." Mrs. M tells Johnny that he will get a zero on the paper; he will serve a detention with her tomorrow night, and she will call his parents later. Johnny, less than pleased, storms out of class and off to lunch.

Mrs. M begins teaching her next class. Meanwhile, Johnny and Suzie go to lunch. At lunch Johnny berates Suzie and bullies her and her friends calling her a "snitch and a liar." He laughs off the detention saying that she is going to be the one that looks stupid and that his mom will get him out of it. Johnny follows up the berating of Suzie with an award-winning tearful phone call to his mother explaining his plight.

He assures his mom that he was not cheating, the teacher hates him, and Suzie is just jealous because she "likes" him and he will not give her the time of day. Johnny is crying so hard he can "barely speak," because he has never been accused of such a harsh thing as cheating and he does not know what to do. Mom is rather upset as "no one from the school has called her" and "no one is going to call her baby a liar." So, she is "on her way to that school to get to the bottom of this."

Meanwhile, Suzie, after being bullied by Johnny, is also on the phone with mom. She is upset because she was not a snitch or a liar. Mrs. M asked her about Johnny, she did not volunteer the information and Johnny was looking at her paper; she saw him. Suzie's mom is rather upset that "she knows nothing about this" and the fact that her baby is being bullied. She, too, is on her way to that school.

A few moments later the school secretary calls the principal to the office as there is a parent waiting in the office to see her. The principal is on lunch duty with only one other administrator and seven hundred students. The principal explains that the parent must wait for the remaining forty minutes until lunch is over. Though the secretary attempts to explain that the principal and assistant principal are tied up, the parent will hear nothing of it, and goes across the street to see the superintendent.

When Johnny's mother arrives at the superintendent's office, he is away at an out-of-town meeting. Johnny's mother demands to see anyone as "someone is going to handle this" and one of the assistant superintendents takes the meeting with the parent. The assistant superintendent has been forced to walk out of another meeting to take this meeting and left six people sitting, but the assistant superintendent "knows this mother" and knows that not taking the meeting will only make this mother madder and will only make matters worse.

While she has no idea why the mother is there this is normal behavior for this family. Johnny's mother explains the distressed phone call that she received from her son and how she needed to leave her job to ensure his safety and wonders what was "being done to him."

She demands answers now and will not leave until she gets them. She is offended that her son was accused of such lies and wants the teacher and the principal who "refused to meet with her" fired immediately. The assistant superintendent calms Johnny's mother and assures her that she will research this and have the building principal call her later, by the end of the day.

Johnny's mother reluctantly leaves, after forty-five minutes of yelling, threatening, and cursing, that "there will be hell to pay if I don't have a call by the end of the day." The assistant superintendent puts a call in to the principal, who is still at lunch duty and leaves a message with her secretary to have her return her call and returns to her meeting where they have been waiting for her.

Meanwhile in the building, lunch duty has ended and the principal has returned to her office. When she returns, expecting that there is a parent waiting for her based on the previous call, she finds out that that parent has gone over to the superintendent's office and that Suzie's mother is here to speak to her. Remember this entire time, Mrs. M is still teaching.

The principal takes the meeting with Suzie's parent assuring her she will talk to Mrs. M and have Mrs. M call her later, returns the call from the assistant superintendent regarding Johnny's mom and her concerns, and speaks to Mrs. M and instructs the teacher to call both mothers, which she intended to do anyway after school.

Mrs. M returns to the principal's office at the end of the day stating that she had spoken to both parents. Suzie's mother understood and appreciated the call, apologized that she did not give Mrs. M a chance to even call before she came to the office, and understood the situation. Johnny's mother on the other hand believes her son, who said that Mrs. M and Suzie were liars, and she said would "sue the school and contact the media if a detention was served and a zero given on a paper."

Subsequently a meeting is set with Mrs. M, the principal, Johnny, and Johnny's mother. The meeting does not end well. The meeting is stopped because Johnny's mother called Mrs. M a selfish bitch who only cares about the popular kids because "she is the cheerleading coach." Johnny's mother refuses to allow him to serve the detention and storms out of the office threating to call the media.

The principal thanks Mrs. M for her time and immediately calls the superintendent to apprise her about what just happened at the parent meeting. The principal explains that, despite trying to find a win-win solution in the meeting, the parent would have no part of it. The only resolution that the parent would hear is that there would be *no* discipline of Johnny because "he said he did not do anything and he would never lie. And the school was not going to get by with such a disgrace as calling her son a liar and cheat."

The superintendent hangs up the phone with the principal and immediately calls the parent to set another meeting and hopefully reach middle ground. In the meantime, Johnny does not have to serve his detention and tells Mrs. M, "My mom said you are a joke and she will get me out of this detention. I told you I would not serve it."

In attendance at the meeting called by the superintendent are the superintendent, the principal, Johnny, Mrs. M, and Johnny's mother. This meeting, though not as nasty, ends with the parent demanding the job of the teacher and threatening lawyers and going to the media if the detention is not removed, the grade given back and the teacher apologizing to Johnny for accusing him of being a liar and a cheat.

The school reiterates that Johnny must serve detention the next day or Johnny will face out of school suspension for cutting the detention. With that the meeting ends with Johnny's mom yelling, "You have not heard the last of this" and Johnny laughs as they leave saying, "I told you, I am not serving a detention." Within two hours, the superintendent's office receives a phone call comes from a local news agency asking about the bullying behavior from a teacher to a student and would like the school to comment.

Let me pause here, while laughing so hard. Every educator that has ever been on the receiving side of a "Johnny's mom" is laughing right now saying, "Yes, been there, done that." Every principal, every assistant principal, every assistant superintendent, and every superintendent is sighing right now saying, "Been there, done that, and this could end very badly for all personnel involved."

And, if you are a parent, you are either saying, "Are you kidding me? This is stupid," or "That's right. Get that school, they can't accuse Johnny of cheating (even though he was)" or "Fight against the system . . . no discipline," or "Suzie should have covered her paper better; Johnny was being resourceful and should not be punished for that." Or "a detention for cheating and a zero? Come on. That is a little harsh now isn't it?" or "What? Only a detention and a zero? Are you kidding me? I mean he bullied Suzie and she did not do anything," or "What about poor Suzie, doesn't she get a voice?" or "This is completely out of hand!"

Every one of those statements is true in the eye of the beholder, but the school has gone from a simple incident that happened between two students in one classroom in their big school building to a media event on the six o'clock news portraying Mrs. M as a bully and the school as evading the press "because they have no comment." So, how does this end? That will be left for you to debate. Here are the facts you must debate.

There is no debate that Johnny cheated off of Suzie regardless of what he told his mother. There is also no debate that this "discipline issue" is out of the hands of the very people who are in the schools hired and equipped to make the decision . . . the teacher and the administrator. Also, what is not in debate is the devastation this decision will have on the teacher, the class, Johnny, Suzie, their parents, the administration, and the school as a whole. So you decide.

This is an actual example that is playing out, right now, as you read this, in every school across the nation, and schools are left knowing that whatever the decision or choice they make, there will be a cost; it will be great, and it will have fallout. The decision becomes not about what is right or wrong. The decision comes down to what the cost will be and whether we can afford it, and how we can minimize the fallout to the rest of the school and the children involved who had nothing to do with this incident. And, don't forget the political sand for all of the administrators involved. Again, you decide.

STORY #2: IT WAS JUST A PRANK

Late spring in a large high school in a rather affluent district, a group of seniors decide to place weed killer on the football field spelling out their graduation year. They complete their task by painting the home bleachers with "Go seniors!" and "We Are Outta here." The damage was done early on a Sunday morning and was not discovered until late Monday afternoon when the mowing crew arrived to mow the infield. The damage was immediately brought to the attention of the athletic director, the assistant principals, the principal, and the superintendents.

The damage and its cost were being quickly assessed as graduation was to be held in those very stands in less than two weeks. Video (though very limited) was being viewed and students were being interviewed. As word of the damage began to permeate through the school, students were beginning to talk, and video and cell phone pictures taken as the damage was being done were circulating around the school. The police have become involved now as this is property damage, and breaking and entering, and a liability issue. The football field gate was locked, and the students had climbed the fence to break in and do the damage.

After a few days of interviews, confiscating phones, looking at video surveillance, and meeting with parents, it was determined that there were five students involved. These were all "good students," who had never really been in trouble before, were about to graduate in a couple of weeks, and who were off to college in the fall. Meeting after meeting was held, carefully getting the written confessions of each of the individuals with their parents admitting that they indeed had done the damage to the school.

Parents were told that disciplinary action would be forthcoming once all students had been met with individually, with their parents, and with the administration. All groups of parents were met with individually and they offered apologies on behalf of their children and offered to pay for the damages. All parents were supportive, in their individual meetings, that their children were out of line, destructive, disrespectful, and were embarrassed by their behavior as they "were raised better than that." All five students were suspended for five days to complete the investigation process, work with the police, and make a decision regarding any further disciplinary actions.

Now let's pause for what is not in debate. All five students did the damage to the football field and the bleachers. All five students admitted, in the presence of their parents and in writing, that they did indeed damage and paint the bleachers and put weed killer in the grass of the football field and water it to make sure it killed the grass. All five admit that they jumped the fence and did this damage.

The cost of repairs is $7,500 and that has been shown to all parents and students. All parents and students understand that their students are going to be suspended, though a couple of the parents have voiced that a suspension is harsh "as it was a joke." The more vocal parents (two sets) begin to meet and discuss that even a suspension of their children is rather harsh as "they have never been in trouble before." But here is where the real dissention comes.

The school decides that they will not press criminal charges, despite the pressure of the local police department to do so, but the students will be suspended for the remainder of the school year (ten more days), they may not walk in graduation, and they will make restitution to the school for the cost to repair the bleachers and the stands. The parents unite, go to the media, and a media story erupts.

Everyone has an opinion and takes a stance on one side of the story or the other. There are the sides that believe that the punishment is ridiculous and harsh while the other side cannot believe that, because of who these kids are, they were allowed to break into the football stadium, damage it and the bleachers and "get away with it." There are those who believe that the students should have gotten in worse trouble, but because they are "the popular kids," they are getting by without more punishment.

Then there are others vocally screaming that "this has gotten out of hand" and the school is "taking it too far." There are wild versions of what actually did happen that become more and more farfetched and the real story seems to be lost. There are versions of the story that some of the students were framed, named by peers, when they were not actually there. There are versions of the story that have the school naming these students, because they "really don't know who did it and need someone to pay for it." There are wild versions that even say that there were more students involved but were never on video; therefore, they are getting away with it. There is meeting after meeting, a firestorm of media, students taking sides, parents fighting, and another no-win for the school.

So, again you decide. Remember what came into play here was not only the school's view on what was "appropriate discipline," but also the parents' philosophy of discipline and what they would have done in their own homes with their own children. The schools are left in the political throes of public opinion regarding discipline and are therefore paralyzed. You see it does not really matter how this discipline situation ended up.

The administration is in a no-win situation regardless of what disciplinary decision they make. Based on the media attention, the community is in an uproar, the students divided, the parents (some very influential) upset, and the educational process at a virtual standstill with only a week left before graduation. The school cannot and will not win this political battle and must make a decision, not on what is right or best, but on how they will restore order and learning to the school as soon as possible. Whether or not you agree with the discipline is not the issue; the issue here has now become one of fear.

Behind the curtain that is being shown here in regard to parents, schools, and discipline are:

1. Every disciplinary decision from the smallest detention to an expulsion comes with political weight, and that political weight must be considered before any decision is made.
2. Every administrator and every teacher has to be prepared to tell the "rest of the story" regarding a disciplinary decision understanding that the parent on the receiving end may not care to hear it.
3. Every school is aware that any disciplinary issue, no matter how small it seemed at the time, is one phone call away from being the lead story on tonight's news—factual or not.
4. Every educator understands that any disciplinary issue can be the reason that they lose their job . . . quickly.
5. Discipline has been, is, and always will be the topic of our discussions until we get to the root of the real issue, and that is a lack of trust!

So, how do we fix this machine called discipline? How can we get together on this one? Boy, that is an issue that is very large, but it starts small. It has to start, just as mentioned in the previous chapter, with trust. We have to learn to trust each other in regard to discipline. We have to admit that, while we may not always agree, we have to come to some understanding. We have to stop reacting against our schools and give them time to handle the situations before "we show up at that school."

We have to stop believing that the schools will have the exact same manner in parenting our children when they are not our children's parents. We must remember that it is not the job of our schools to parent; it is the job of our schools to educate. We must support our schools and the decisions that they make in regard to discipline. We must support our schools at home by supporting that discipline, rather than attacking the school in front of our child so they can return to school tomorrow repeating that to the teacher or the administrators.

We have to treat each other with common courtesies. That includes not cursing at each other or showing up at our child's school demanding that the world be dropped because you have arrived and are mad. We have to learn to respect the time and the feelings of those who are in our schools; they are humans, too. We have to stop utilizing the media to "tell our story" when we are angry and perhaps not being rational in the moment.

We must not allow the media's definition of our schools to be "reality." We must unite, circle, and protect the image and reputation of our schools and the precious commodities in them, our teachers and our students. We must develop a partnership with our children's teachers and schools in regards to the behaviors of our children and work with the school to increase learning for everyone. After all, together we are unstoppable.

Curtain #26

Together, There Are Steps to Fix the Parent versus School Crisis

Schools and parents can make learning and teaching powerful when the relationship is healthy, open, honest, transparent, and is grounded in trust and communication. Schools must have this sort of relationship with families in order for the system as a whole to work toward the common goal of educating our students and making them successful.

Frustrations from parents toward their children's schools have reached an all-time high at both ends of the spectrum. The collaborative sense of partnership between a school and some parents has given way to an accusatory attack of words, in a conflict playing out right in front of our vulnerable children.

In the previous chapter about parenting, let's add some very simple do's and don'ts that every single teacher and administrator would love to say to each and every parent out there but knows better if they want to keep their job. It is with confidence and knowledge that after reading this we, as parents who care about our schools, can make a difference in our schools.

We, the very parents of the students in our buildings can begin to change the direction and the attacks on our schools. We, as stakeholders in the schools across these great states, can begin to see what is happening in our schools as positive, beneficial, necessary and valuable for their lives. We have to begin the dialogues, we must stop the attacks and gossiping, we have to check the negative chatter, and we must build a community of support around our schools.

Now, I'll hit the pause button before going any further and reiterate that this part is *not* speaking to every single person who has ever borne a child and sent them off to school. Not every parent who has ever had a child in school is a part of the problem; rather, many are the solution. And, before every person who has ever spawned a child throws this book at me or whoever else is closest screaming, “How dare she say that!” let me say this: if the shoe fits . . . and if it doesn’t fit then calm down and read on.

The purpose of this final summation of do’s and don’ts in regard to our schools is not to attack, but to pull down the curtain and expose what it is doing to our school and how this poisonous, contentious relationship is breaking the system. One final comment while we are paused. Yes, as a parent, you have a right to go to your child’s school and talk to whomever you want. No one is arguing your ability, your right, your desire, and your time to “go to that school whenever you want.” The curtain that must be pulled back is the cost to our schools. So, release the pause button and here are simple do’s and don’ts that most educators want you to know but know better than to tell you.

OPEN AND HONEST COMMUNICATION IS CRITICAL

Open and honest communication is a must. Schools and parents should feel as if they are in a relationship with only one item on the agenda. The only item on the agenda must be the successful graduation of the child. Walking through every grade level and every class from kindergarten to senior English are all steps on the ladder, but the end goal is to graduate from high school armed with the tools to move on to the next step of the child’s post-secondary journey. Here are a few words every educator would love to say to parents in regard to what open and honest communication looks like.

Do communicate with your child’s teacher, administrator, or school if you have any questions. Make a call. Send an e-mail. Ask questions. Attend meetings. Visit the Web site.

Don’t (unless it is an extreme emergency) send threatening e-mails or leave long damning voicemails. These kinds of e-mails and voicemails only put the school on the defensive from an attack and do nothing to bridge the gap in the issues as a parent you are experiencing.

Don’t show up to the school demanding to see the teacher or speak to the principal unannounced. The teacher is teaching and cannot leave the classroom to deal with your concern no matter how important you feel it is. No parent would appreciate it if the teacher left their child unattended to meet with a parent and you should not ask that for your child. Administrators’ days are full and often overscheduled. What they are doing most is visiting the classrooms of your children’s teachers and dealing with the daily running and safety of the building.

Every administrator values meetings with and spending time with parents. Administrators are ready, willing, and able to address concerns at any *sched-*

uled meeting you would like, however often you would like. But, to show up at your child's school demanding that the administrator see you immediately is neither respectful nor helpful. Often, they will have to cancel another meeting that may have already been scheduled (perhaps with another parent), and no one benefits. The administrator is unprepared, the teacher is unaware, and nothing beneficial will happen at that meeting other than you, as a parent, venting your concerns. The teacher or the administrator will still have to investigate the situation, schedule another meeting, and get back with you.

Do expect that your phone calls or e-mails to the teacher or the administrator should be responded to within twenty-four hours (as long as the teacher or administrator is not absent from school) but *do not* call a teacher or an administer in the evening when you are angry demanding that "you had better return this call first thing in the morning or I am coming up to that school." Again, if the teacher gets the message first thing when they arrive and does not have a prep period until one o'clock in the afternoon that is when you will receive a return call, and coming up to the school, demanding to see that teacher will only frustrate you and benefit no one. Likewise, for any administrator, you should expect in most cases a return call within twenty-four hours.

Let's pause here when speaking about communication and say this: e-mails are sometimes the best way of communication, but can often be the worst. Nothing replaces the good old face-to-face meeting because tone and intent are open to the interpretation of the receiver when you send an e-mail or a text. You e-mail facts, but you have conversations. There could be an entire book written with the litany of threatening, name-calling, accusatory, disrespectful e-mails that have been sent to principals and teachers alike.

Many people have become ten feet tall and bullet proof behind an e-mail, saying things they would never say to anyone's face. Schools are no different. In regard to written communication with your child's teacher and/or school, keep the e-mail short, factual, and request a meeting to share all of the "details." Sending a lengthy e-mail stating "what better happen," or "what you will do" or "what is not going to happen," or "I will do, if you don't," does no one any good. It will not get you what you want, and it will put the receiver on the defensive.

Do remember that communication involves all parties involved. The story that your child told you when they came home from school or explained to you when you asked why they did not do well on that test is only one side of the story. There is another side and you must hear it before drawing any conclusions. Make sure that you hear the other side of the story.

Let me offer this analogy here. If we were coming down the highway on different sides of the roads heading in the opposite direction when an accident happened in front of us, we would give the police two different stories. Neither of us is wrong or lying about the accident. We simply had two completely different vantage points as we came to the accident from two completely different angles. The same is true of what happened in class today or why the test grade was not good. There are two vantage points: the student's and the teacher's. *Do* hear both sides and *don't* judge the situation until you have "seen the accident" from both points of view.

One more thing that must be added here in regard to communication via e-mail or text is name calling and accusations. No matter how frustrated you are and no matter if you call later and apologize because "you were angry," they are never acceptable. After receiving countless phone calls as both a teacher and as an administrator, parents often "apologized for sending or saying" later. They just "were angry and should have not said/written those things."

Regardless of how frustrated and angry you are, the teachers and administrators you are referring to are educated, intelligent, hardworking, dedicated, and devoted individuals who never, under any circumstances, deserve to be at the receiving end of your frustrations and anger. So, when you are getting ready to hit send, please, pause, reflect, and remember this paragraph before you do. The person on the other end of your rant is your child's teacher or your child's administrator. They are human beings, and they have memories and feelings. They deserve more.

So, the summation regarding communication is this: Schools are willing and able to communicate with parents and welcome that communication and often thrive on it, but, what must be remembered here is that in the classroom no matter where your son sits, he is your son, and to you there is no one more important, but the same is equally true for each and every other parent who has a child sitting in that room of thirty-plus students.

The teacher must balance the needs of all of his or her students, not just the one. All parents would expect consideration for their child and schools want you to understand that they must take all parents' desires into consideration; therefore, you must remember that when it comes to communication, "An ounce of sugar goes much further than a pint of vinegar."

TRUST IS A MUST

This has been said a couple of times, but it is a big *do* for making our schools more collaborative. One of the toughest things for every parent to understand is that the experience that their child is having or has had with education is often clouded by their own experiences as children themselves. If, as a child, a parent had a bad teacher, or a mean administrator, or was suspended from school or even expelled, their "view" of education will be skewed and that "view" will be manifested to their child.

The statement of, "Well, I never did very well in blank class, so I am not surprised they are not either" is one that has been heard from any teacher who has been in the classroom for more than one day as an excuse for their child's errors. Or the statement that "I never liked school or my teachers, and I tell my son that all the time." If we pass that "baggage" on to our children, it is no wonder why the system is broken in the aspect of parent-school communication.

Do trust your child's school, and *don't* place *your* baggage at the footsteps of your child's teacher or administration. *Do*, as human beings, assume that the very people in our schools are there with a good heart and good intent. *Do* begin to look at situations that will arise with questions rather than attacks. *Do* build a relationship as parents and schools that is built on the foundation of knowing that the people running our schools and teaching our classes are honest, good-hearted people who want the best for the children they are leading or teaching and not monsters that need to be berated and attacked at every possible opportunity.

Do speak of our schools and our teachers as if we respect and value them. *Do not* participate in the latest round of gossip or attack on the news this evening. *Do not* attack our teachers and schools in front of our children. Those attacks divide us and do nothing to bring us together. *Do* learn how to question and ask about our concerns trusting that the very people teaching our children know and want the best for them, regardless of our own personal experience.

Trust between parents and schools is the cornerstone for fixing the broken system that exists within many of our schools. If we can all, parents, teachers, and administrators, come to the table with a collaborative supportive heart there is no limit to what we can accomplish. There is no issue we cannot resolve. There is no height we cannot achieve. There is no amount of love that cannot be given to our children. We must trust each other and begin with the idea that everyone is coming to the table with good intent and with the best interests of the child in their hearts. Together trust must be built.

ENGAGEMENT IS VITAL

One of the largest frustrations of schools is the engagement of parents, or what feels like a lack of engagement from parents to schools. Schools have gone to exorbitant expense and time in communicating with parents. There are now Web sites, text messages, Facebook groups, Twitters, e-mails, phone calls, newsletters, and a myriad of other methods that schools are utilizing to attempt to keep parents in the "know" about what is happening in their children's schools.

Schools are very aware that parents are busy and therefore utilize various sources of communication multiple times. Many schools also have school messenger systems that send out automated texts and calls; however, as a parent you must sign up for them. Also, many schools have school data systems, on which parents can access a teacher's grade book and see their child's grades (homework, quizzes, tests, and classwork) live and as often as they want to. Some schools also now provide parent-access to teachers' lesson plans and materials distributed in class to additionally communicate with parents what is happening in their children's classrooms on a daily, weekly, and monthly basis. Admittedly, some schools are better communicators than others and some may not use every form of communication that has been spoken of but they are certainly using some communication.

But, here is where engagement is vital: As a parent you must do your part. So, the *do* is this . . . be engaged in your child's education. How?

- *Do* sign on with the school for whatever school messaging system they have and read those messages. Remember, sometimes messages sent out are grade or class specific, so if you talk to another parent who got a message you did not, ask about the message or class and make sure you should have gotten it in the first place. *Do not* assume ignorance in regard to this form of communication. It is there and provided for parents, so use it.
- *Do* get the password for your child's school data warehouse and check the grades of your child often. Follow your student's learning through every medium your school offers. If you have access to teachers' lesson plans, look at them and discuss what is happening in your child's classroom. Look over your student's grades and communicate with the teacher if there are any discrepancies or question regarding what your student is saying in the classroom and what you are seeing on the school-wide data system or lesson plans. *Do not* assume it is the school's responsibility to communicate with you about what is happening in the classroom every day. They will reach out if the situation is extreme, but that can often be too late. They are the teacher's children to educate; they are your children, as parents, to raise.
- *Do* attend meetings that are held at the school. We are all busy, but no educator would be staying later into the evening and holding any meeting without a need to share and disseminate information. *Do not* claim ignorance after the information has been shared at a meeting. Not attending a meeting *does not* negate parents from the responsibility of knowing what is happening in their child's class or school.
- *Do* speak positively of your school. When issues arise address them head on and immediately. *Do not* gossip and talk about "what that school did or did not do," especially in front of the student.

- *Do*, if a concern, a question, or an issue comes up regarding a grade, a project, a test, a class homework assignment, or anything else that happens in the classroom, contact the teacher first. That includes a story that your child may have told you about "what happened in class today." Reach out to the teacher to understand rather than accuse. *Do not* call the administrator first to air a complaint. If you choose to call the administrator first you are only guaranteeing two things:

    1. There are two people on the phone together who do not know what the facts are (the parent and the principal), because neither person was in the room.
    2. The parent will indeed need to speak to the teacher regarding the concern.

- *Do* request a meeting with the teacher, the administration, or the school in advance. Sometimes even after an e-mail or a phone call there still seems to be an issue. *Do not* hesitate to reach out to the school to get all parties involved (the student, the parent, the teacher, and the administrator) around the same table to brainstorm ideas to resolve the issue.
- *Do* come to that table with an open and willing heart to hear and listen to how, together, the issue can be solved. *Do not* come prepared to accuse and to attack.

ATTACKS ARE DAMAGING

No one benefits from an attack. It is completely understandable how protective we all are in regard to our children. Schools understand the protective nature of parents is no different than a lioness protecting her threatened cubs. Remember, most educators are parents themselves; but what is being lost is the manner in which we are attacking. The attacks that have been witnessed by me personally from parents are personal in nature, threatening, and are completely out of hand.

We must remember that the people in that school are humans and must be treated as such. *Do not* come to school and threaten schools. No one wins with threats. *Do* come to school with an open heart searching to understand and to find a solution. *Do not* pass your bad experience of education on to those educating your child. They are not your former teacher or principal, and they do not deserve it.

Let me share this story with you. As a new principal, I observed parents bypassing the main office and going straight to a teacher's classroom to talk to them. This policy shocked me, yet it did not seem to bother anyone else.

The explanation given to me when asked was that "these parents have been doing this for years and you are not going to stop it now."

My previous experience was in a very large school where such freedoms would never be permitted. No parent was allowed to just walk into the building without signing in and being escorted to where they were going. Most of the parents in my previous buildings had understood that need for security and safety for their children's building, but there was an assurance given to me saying "that was not the way it was here." It was appalling to me and therefore a change in that policy began immediately.

We immediately communicated to parents that they must stop in the office and be escorted to wherever they wanted to go. More shocking than that, parents had to be notified that they would no longer be escorted to the classroom of a teacher who was teaching. Parents had to be told that if a teacher is teaching that teacher would not be interrupted unless in extreme emergencies. This did not go over well, but for the most part those concerns were addressed through e-mails, explaining the logic and reasoning and most, but not all parents, began to understand.

After a few weeks of the new policy being in place some parents would come to sign in, but, depending on who they were, say, "I don't need an escort" and leave the office to head wherever they wanted to go. This *was* happening without my knowledge.

One day, a parent rather upset with her child's teacher, bypassed the office, went right upstairs, knocked on a teacher's door and began screaming at the teacher regarding a grade. Mind you, there was an entire room full of students who were in that classroom, but not the child of the parent who was in the hallway. The parent continued to become even more vocal until a teacher whose room was close to them came out in the hallway to see what all of the commotion was about and alerted the office.

One of the assistant principals and I went upstairs to the sound of the parent yelling and screaming at the teacher. Students were in the halls, other teachers were closing their classroom doors, and instruction was being interrupted. It took several minutes for us to talk the parent into leaving the hallway and coming to the office. She complied, and we spent the next hour trying to understand what the grading issue was in the first place.

An explanation was given to her by me that she could not just enter that building and do what she had done, and then she attacked. All reason was lost on her, there was no rationalizing with her, and we had to escort her from the building with the assistance of security.

There could be another entire chapter written on the litany of meetings that took place after this, but here is the point: That "attack" got no one anywhere. The teacher felt attacked, students were at risk, administrators were caught off guard, and the child whose grade was in question was not assisted in understanding the material better.

It is without question to me that some of you reading this are saying, "Oh, come on, that is so farfetched. I mean, she was crazy. That would not happen in most schools and on most days." If you believe that, you are so sadly mistaken.

Administrators have witnessed parents with guns enter buildings looking for a teacher, a student, or an administrator. Administrators have watched parents be hauled off to jail for attacking a teacher or an administrator. Administrators have watched fights break out in offices with a parent who was not pleased with what the school was telling them. Administrators have called security and told them to stand in or close to a parent meeting when the parent was perceived as adversarial. This is happening every day in every school and our students are sitting in those schools.

Let's finish this section by saying that in order to fix this part of the broken system, attacks must stop, period.

SUCCESS IS FOR EVERYONE

The final thought that must be elaborated here in regard to parents' involvement in trying to fix our schools is that everyone is working toward a common goal. Schools have to become more flexible in dealing with what mandates and changes are thrown at them, and parents must understand that education is different than when they were in school. The tired old statements of "Well, that is the way we learned in school and I have done just fine in life" is not acceptable anymore. "The way we learned before" is not the way that this generation of students learns now.

Everyone must remember that the very people in front of classes today and in buildings are far more versed and far more able to teach than most of us without that training would be. It would seem ludicrous, to most of us, to walk into a mechanic's garage and tell him how to change tires, and it would seem silly to walk into a hairdresser's salon and tell her how to cut hair. Most of us do not have the training, knowledge, or ability to do that. Yet, too many parents believe that since "they went to school themselves" that makes them a teacher. Or, if they work in an industry such as science, for example, that they know how to teach chemistry.

We must remember that, while some of us may have much experience in working in and around schools, we are not the highly qualified teacher or administrator running our children's classrooms or schools. We must learn to respect the profession. We must believe that teaching and learning is good no matter what our experience with it was. We must accept that just because we sat in a classroom as a student once and were taught by a teacher, that does not make us a teacher or give us the ability, the skill set, or the knowledge to teach. Here's an example of how out of hand some parents' views as to "how they can run the school" have gotten.

Several years ago, as a principal, one of the assistant principals and I engaged in a conversation regarding how lockers were assigned. Students' lockers were assigned by grade rather than by location of their class in the middle of the day and curiosity had me wondering why that was. This was a benign casual conversation held in the hallway between two administrators. There was in no way, shape, or form any suggestion made on either of our parts that lockers be changed, nor was there any suggestion made that there was even going to be a change. It was simply a conversation of inquiry to understand.

A few days later the superintendent at the time called asking why everyone was having their lockers assigned by alphabetical order. Since clearly the conversation that had occurred several days before had been forgotten as it was just a passing conversation, for the life of me I could not understand what he was talking about. Later that day, while standing in the cafeteria on lunch duty with the assistant principal, I described the whole conversation with the superintendent as perplexing. How had that rumor gotten out there? After sharing the conversation with her, she laughed and reminded me of our hallway conversation the other day.

What had happened was a student overheard our conversation (or at least a part of it), went home and repeated it to their parent. The parent bypassed me as building principal and called the superintendent, hence the phone call questioning the decision (or lack thereof one) to change lockers. So, what is the point here? The point has nothing to do with lockers. It has to do with this: We must believe that everyone in the school buildings has the success of all students in their hearts. Moving lockers, not moving lockers, changing schedules, moving teachers, offering classes, or not offering classes are done with everyone in the school looking at the bigger picture: ensuring success for all.

We must, as people who know that the very people in our schools can and do have the best interest of our students at heart, let educators do their jobs. We must get out of the way and give up the feeling that we have some sort of right, because our child attends school there, to be involved in decisions that are made for the best interest of the whole school—not just our child. We must stop threatening our schools and making them so fearful of repercussions that they are afraid to make any decision, including those that they know are best for our students.

We must join together as parents, students, administrators, and stakeholders to support and to understand. We must agree that, while we may not believe in every decision that is made in our schools, we do believe that everyone in those schools has the success of students in their hearts. We must begin to move together as a united front rather than continuing the attacking, gossiping, divisive manners in which we are treating our schools to fix our school system.

Curtain #27

The Most Important Voices Are Not Being Heard

Move every political maneuvering out of the way, push aside all state testing, ignore all teachers and administrators, and what you have left are the most important people in every school building, our children, but their voices have been silenced by all of the deafening noise of the fighting and yelling and political grandstanding. Their hearts are not heard, their voices are quieted by what is happening both at home and in their schools.

Our students of today are not the students of yesteryear. Shoot, our students of today are not the students of yesterday. Students are learning in a completely different timeframe, with completely different tools, in completely different manners, and with completely different stimuli than most of us can imagine. Students of today are living in homes that are vastly different than those most of us grew up in, and with very different values and priorities than those with which we were raised. Expectations have grown loftier, the cost of the education has gotten higher, and the pressures to learn have become almost too much for many to bear.

Our schools are simply not equipped to handle what our students (or many of them) need from us. So, since we are not able to handle every situation, we fail them. Schools are not failing students due to any form of mean-spirited antics; they are just able to deal with the vast majority of issues in one room, at one time, in one year and still teach the curriculum (and perhaps prepare for a state test). Before there is a revolt from schools, here is an explanation.

OUR "BROKEN" STUDENTS ARE NOT HEARD

Students who have severe issues of profound abuse, abandonment, separation, and such, cannot learn. A student who was burned last night by a parent, or molested over the weekend by an uncle, or whose parents announced they were divorcing over break is not equipped or prepared to learn math or read their textbook today. Schools are forced to hire and offer more social worker and mental health support than ever before. Schools are counseling families and parents so that children can learn, and teachers, who did not go to school to become counselors, are doing the best they can but are ill equipped in dealing with such deep levels of anger and pain.

Schools are working with more and more "broken" children without the tools and the talents to repair them. Remember, for most of us reading this, school is where we went to *learn*. We got love, support, encouragement, and value from those in our lives outside our schools, but this does not ring true for every child in our classrooms and schools today. Please understand every educator's complete understanding and heart-wrenching for the pain of our children and the need for those "broken" children to be educated. Educators also are very clear that most of the "brokenness" that has come to those children was no choice of their own. The point being made here is that that "brokenness" is met in school without the proper tools and abilities to make students whole again.

Schools are triaging the crisis, but they are not equipped to truly deal with the issues, so for too many of our children, they are just moved on to the next teacher or grade with little assistance in-between. Schools are not equipped to deal with families in crisis; they may not even know that families are in crisis and what to do or not to do, and the child gets lost in the shuffle.

Every administrator has listened to one after another heart-wrenching story from students. We have felt their pain. We have wiped their tears. We have offered what supports we had and what assistance we knew of, but we knew we were only putting a Band-Aid on what was a gaping wound. We have felt the sense that we were not offering this child what they needed to be "fixed" enough to learn.

We, as educators, knew that we were doing the best with what we had to offer but what we went to school to do was to learn to teach not counsel. We knew the issues that many of our students had were far out of our expertise and knowledge to fix them. We knew that we were not helping and in some instances doing a disservice by not helping. We were simply lost in the limited opportunities we had at our fingertips to assist.

We watched as families were broken due to drug and alcohol abuse and offered what supports we had, but knew that often we were sending the child right back to the very home that was causing the "brokenness" with little we could do. There were countless times when we called child protective services on various situations brought to us by our teachers that we knew we were not "fixing" the child and might, depending on the outcome, be hurting them.

We have felt the anger and the frustration knowing that we were not helping some children to graduate from high school because the issues they were dealing with were far too serious for them to even see past today, let alone graduation day. We have, along with our colleagues, felt this responsibility, this pain, this loss, this anger, this frustration, this emptiness, for our broken children.

THOSE IN THE "MIDDLE" GET LOST

Many school mandates and school monies are provided to assist struggling or behind grade-level students. There is often quite of bit of money offered, depending on the students, to assist those students who are behind grade-level or who are not passing the state tests. Every school is very aware of these monies and will utilize them to assist struggling students. There is also additional funding that comes from most states to assist the best and brightest. There are monies that are provided to offer additional college-readiness classes and preparation for the best and the brightest in our schools.

If you look at most schools and total the students at both the lowest end and the top end, they would total about 35 percent of the entire student population. Remember, as mentioned, for most schools in most states there are funds to support the learning and gaps that the lowest in our schools need in regard to remediation and appropriate-level preparedness. There are also additional funds provided to our schools to assist the best and the brightest in achieving at higher levels.

Just as an average according to that math (and that math will vary from school to school depending on its location and socioeconomic situation) that leaves 65 percent of the student population "in the middle" where there are no additional resources or time. There are no additional funds to assist those, who, in most schools, are the vast majority of our students. The vast majority of students just move through our system.

They are passed on from grade to grade, teacher to teacher, and class to class. These students are often not in trouble much and either have a supportive home life or have learned how to "fake it" to push through what they have to do to graduate and move on in their lives. They are what schools must know are the silent ones with few voices who just move through our systems and are lost. They are lost because they are often not given the supports they may need. They come to school either prepared or not but have learned enough and are smart enough to make it through their classes and to get the grade.

They are not the brightest students, but they are not struggling to pass either. They are not failing classes or requiring any remediation, nor are they achieving at a high level. They are often described and labeled as "having such potential" yet carry through day after day going through their day. They are not lost in our system due to any malice or bad intention, they are just lost, or, better said, not supported as well as they could or should be.

THE PRESSURE HAS GOTTEN SO HIGH

There was once a day that existed in school when going to college and preparing to go to college was a desire—a dream, not something that one was pressured to do. There was never the feeling that if college was not the chosen path, one would not find success in life. Not all youth attended college yet they are doing just fine. But, for today's students, it is not that way.

Schools have so much pressure on them to prepare our graduating seniors to enter the workforce or college that we begin those conversations as early as middle school. We are pigeonholing twelve- to fourteen-year-olds to make a decision as to what they want to do with the rest of their lives. For certain there are some forty-year-olds who do not know how to answer that question.

Schools are under the gun from both local and federal legislation to show college and career readiness programs. Schools must demonstrate that they are preparing students for "college and career readiness," which often looks like pushing them into career decisions that they are not ready to make at their age.

We are being forced to shove our children into those boxes so early on, without knowing fully if they will fit. Rather than graduating from high school with the broad knowledge base to move forward as an eighteen-year-old at least more equipped to make that decision with a wide variety of choices, we are "tracking" our students by pushing them into fields they may or may not be ready for. Let me give you a couple of examples.

Right now, without question, there are students taking classes at a coordinating vocational school to be fire fighters. If you asked them, "So, I guess you are excited to graduate and become a firefighter?" the student would laugh and say, "No, it was the only vocational class that was still open when I turned in my application."

Again, right now there is a student taking a college class offered at the high school and not doing well at it. If they were asked, "Why are you taking this college class as you are not doing too well?" the student would respond, "So that I can leave the other three days of the week early from school." While success in college or vocational opportunities may drive some students, it is not the driving force for many.

Both are decisions being made by voices too young to really know what they wanted and what they needed based on their age. Yet, schools, and therefore parents, are feeling that pressure to graduate students from high school prepared to walk into their "forever" right after high school. Schools know that in order to meet the federal and state guidelines they must enroll a percentage of their students in college classes. Schools are feeling pressured to place students in the classes that they may not want to take or may not even need later in their lives.

The latest study states that this generation of high school graduates will change careers seven to ten times before they retire. If that is a true statement, why are we forcing twelve- to fourteen-year-olds to graduate in a "forever career" that they will never keep or not preparing them for careers that may not even exist right now?

We have begun pushing careers on our students earlier and earlier in their educational journeys. We now have middle school students taking high school classes so that high school students can take college classes. We are beginning in grade school to push students to look at "what they want to be when they grow up" due to the pressures that schools are feeling from the new federal mandates to graduate students who are career and college ready, whether they really are or not.

Did you know exactly what you wanted to do with the rest of your life when you were in grade school? How about middle school? Were you ready in high school to begin taking college courses? Many of us would laugh that, as adults, some of us are still struggling with that question, but we are demanding it of our students earlier and earlier.

This curtain is one that is hanging due to mandated requirements and not what is always in the best interest of the child. Are there children who are ready early? Of course. So, to every parent of every overachieving child who has successfully completed high school credits in middle school and graduated high school with even an associate's degree, calm down.

There is no statement being made here saying that schools should not offer those choices for those students who are ready. The curtain is being pulled back to show that schools are being forced, even pressured, to offer and push more and more students onto a path that they may not be ready to take. At what cost?

THE VOICE OF STUDENT LEARNING HAS BEEN LOST

With all of the political maneuvering, the teacher evaluation arguments, the state testing, and the school board and administration power plays, students' voices are getting lost. No one is asking students what they need. Their voices are not included in any decision that involves their learning because "they are kids," and all of us accept that. Really, how can a six-year-old possibly know what they need to learn? What is lost is the idea that their learning is what is most important. Learning as more than reading and completing math equations but learning as:

- Lifelong learners
- Problem solvers
- Communicators
- Team players
- Collaborative learners
- Task drivers

The ugliest truth in regard to our students' voices is the reality that every student in every school has a price tag on their head. Schools are, based on the individual states and how that state's taxes are being tallied, receiving monies for each and every student in their school, every year. It is sad, but there are schools that know that and are keeping students there for that money. Let me tell you this so you understand this curtain: your student, depending on the school, will be suspended after the state count day (the day that your state department collects the number of students enrolled in your school) and will be brought back to school before that next count day to ensure that the school will receive all of the tax dollars that that student could give.

This is not a statement stating that the majority of our schools are doing this, but make no mistake, it is happening. As embarrassing as it is to say as an administrator, student suspensions would be "held up" if it were close to count day and expulsions held until after count day, and let me tell you the decision to do so was not made in isolation and was encouraged to be made. Money and tax dollars that the student would bring were often critical in deciding when and if they left the school system. Every administrator reading this section will deny that this statement is true, but sadly, in some cases, it is.

With that "price tag" in play, it is no wonder why some of our students become chess pieces moved about the game called school to aid and to assist the schools. It is not shocking to anyone involved in school budgeting that schools must learn to play the game if they would like to keep their doors open at all. Remember, as has been mentioned previously, if they are at the top of the class or needing additional resources there is even more monies that can be gained from those students but at what cost?

This chapter will not be belabored as this chapter among all of them is without question the most sensitive. Here are some thoughts as to how we can begin to resolve the needs of our students.

- We must look at what a "typical" classroom has begun to look like and how we can offer the supports needed for every student's voice.
- We must devise a plan and a manner in which we can listen to what students need while giving them what they must have . . . an education.
- We must look at what we are asking of our students both inside and outside of school and remember that they are children, and it is the adult's job to teach them.
- We must look at our "broken" students and how we can assist them outside of school so that they can come to school prepared to learn.
- We must monitor, watch, advise, and carefully guide the "middle" of our student population as they are our majority and have individual needs of their own.
- We must look at schools as opportunities to offer a wide variety of learnings and experiences, rather than pigeonholing students into careers and directions they may not be ready to take.
- We must support our students by providing the resources to our schools that may be necessary. These are resources that were not necessary years ago but have now become the cornerstone of what our students need. These resources include drug and alcohol prevention and intervention, parenting classes, social workers, psychologists, therapists, counselors, and any other needed services as defined by the school and its population.
- We must differentiate our offerings in our schools to suit the needs of our students, and offer college classes to those who want or need them, remedial classes for those who need them, and exploratory classes for those who are unsure and need to check out the options that might be available to them.
- We must supply schools with the necessary funding to offer these services and to educate the whole child to become a productive, tax-paying member of society once they graduate from high school.

Conclusion

Curtain Call

Whew! Just whew. I feel like throwing my hands up in the air and screaming "Alleluia." Just as after a great church service there is a feeling of coming clean from the "sins of the father" and being cleansed and freed. I have an overwhelming urge to dance across a room and hug each and every person who has read this book and say, thank you for reading this and being a part of what will become a movement of change. Let me also say this:

To every educator who reads this book . . . know you are loved, know you are felt, know you are valued, and know you are supported.

To every parent, grandparent, aunt, or uncle who has read this book, let me say this: We can do better, we can do more, we can make our schools better, we have to do better. Our children, our grandchildren, our nieces, and nephews are counting on us to do better. We must be a part of the solution and never again a part of the problem.

To every school administrator reading this book let me say this: We must lead our buildings, free from the fear of repercussions and lead with the integrity and knowledge we were blessed to have. We are the leadership that will change our schools and prayerfully this book will offer you the courage and the insights to begin conversations to change it.

To every person reading this book who is thinking about entering education or who is in school training to be an educator let me say this: You are the future of education. You must educate as our students need and demand and not as we "have always done it." You are the future of this amazing field and we educators stand confident that built on trust and respect you will move our educational system into the next generation.

Finally, to everyone reading this book who is not "in" education let me say this: support your schools. Give back your schools. Get behind your schools. Be a part of the solutions regarding education not a divisive member. Work with your schools by volunteering, mentoring, educating, and supporting them. Trust them and believe that you can be either a part of the solutions or a part of the problem. It is your choice.

As was said in the opening chapter of this book, the goal in writing this book was to begin a dialogue. We must all move from the blame game to looking at how, together, we can fix the problems in our schools. We must stop pointing fingers and start making movements to better our schools. Together it can happen once we all understand what is happening in our schools and how we can begin to fix it.

When this book began, I never claimed that all of the answers would be found in these pages but this is true: Until that the curtain is pulled back we can't begin to see and discuss the necessary, and sometimes uncomfortable ugliness in our schools, and we can never begin to fix them. We must tell our truth and stand in the light in order to fix our system.

The goal in writing this book was to say what, as has been mentioned in the first chapter, every educator knows and is afraid to say about what is happening in our schools across this nation. The hope is that by pulling back the curtain and letting everyone see "the dirty laundry" behind the door we can pick it up, sort it out, and begin working together to clean it up.

The system is broken, but it can be fixed. There is no error too bad, no decision too awful, and no change that cannot be made if we, together, demand that it be made. We can and must fix our broken system if we ever want to get better. We can no longer rely on "good enough" or "that is the way it has always been" anymore. We must unite and have the uncomfortable conversations that are necessary to fix the system.

We will not all agree but we must begin to move forward in making the system whole again. We must stop all of the arguing, the political grandstanding, the pontificating, the dragging through the mud, the accusations, the attacks, the name calling, the blaming, the ranting, the hiding, and the shame. We have to stop wondering why we are in the position we are and learn to ask and lean on the very people in the trenches, our educators, to fix it.

How? How you say? Well, below are some starting points for discussion. Below are the insights and resolutions from one educator who has built her career on this wonderful, mixed up, confused, and rewarding field we call education. Below are the summations of what every educator knows that, with the right intent, we can create a firestorm of conversations with politicians, teachers, administrators, and parents to move our educational system to where it needs to be . . . forward!

STOP THE POLITICAL GRANDSTANDING

Knowing that even as these words are typed there will be those cynics who are saying, "Come on, Cathy, there are politics everywhere and you think education will be different?" The response is that it has to be. Education has to be different because it is the foundation of what we do. It is, by its very essence, who we are. If the educational system remains broken, then in reality, so do we. If we are not preparing our youngest and brightest, if we are not educating our most vulnerable and most afflicted then what is the point really? If we are not educating our next generation of doctors, nurses, lawyers, and yes, teachers, then what are we doing anyway?

The reference to the political grandstanding includes everyone from Washington, DC, to our local school boards. We must stop utilizing education as a platform for election and to achieve our own personal agendas. We must stop standing on the backs of our schools to gain footing in any form of election. We have to stop. We cannot continue to push our agendas at the cost of our schools and our educators.

There must be a united front in the world of education and we (stakeholders and educators) must work together to find solutions and fix our broken system. As the old saying goes, united we stand and divided we fall. When it comes to where we are right now in regards to our school, we all know, we are falling. We are falling so fast that other nations, who once revered our education system are laughing at us. We cannot continue to work against each other and we must begin to work together for everyone involved.

ADMINISTRATORS MUST BE PROPERLY EXPERIENCED AND ALLOWED TO LEAD

We must demand that the very people put in our schools to lead them are given the freedom to lead and have the experience to do so. We cannot continue to treat our administrators as puppets in the political agendas of our school boards. We must demand appropriate training for our school leaders, force them to continue professional development to remain current on educational trends, and support, not attack them.

These educational leaders must be provided the support and the belief that they have the ability to run our schools. Stakeholders cannot continue to force their own beliefs of "the way it should be" or "the way it has always been" onto our schools. If we want to be better, than we must do better by our students.

They are not learning the way that we did "all those years ago," and schools today are "not what they used to be." And, that is okay. Schools must be allowed to evolve in a new day and a new time, free from the fear of damnation from stakeholders who are afraid to grow and change. We must get out of the way of our school administrators and allow them to lead their buildings.

I have not suggested that school leaders be given a carte blanche ticket to do whatever they wish. What I have suggested is that school administrators be held accountable for the success or the failure of their schools. They should be held accountable and their employment be evaluated as to the success of their teachers and ultimately their students. There is no question that if indeed an administrator is allowed to lead, with experience, with added professional development and support, and free of the political agendas, there will be changes in our schools.

Stakeholders must allow our school leaders to lead the very buildings they were hired to lead. We must support them, hold them accountable, demand experience, and be willing to pay for it, evaluate their success and their failures by offering our support and our resources, and work together as a team toward their success.

WE MUST SUPPORT OUR TEACHERS, EVALUATE THEM APPROPRIATELY, PAY THEM, AND REMOVE "BAD" TEACHERS

Ah, our teachers. The very heart of our schools. After all of the politics, the administrators, the parents, and the community, at the hearts of our schools are our teachers and their students. The very lifeblood of our schools is effective teachers. The one dynamic of any successful building from the most expensive to the run-down building in the center of town is effective teachers. At the core of every great, experienced school attended by our children or every nightmare story on the news tonight is a teacher. There is no single greater commodity, no better resource, no more valuable gem, no greater good, no single determining factor than a teacher.

So, if we all know that, we must demand more and give more to those gems, those wonderful commodities, those amazing resources . . . our teachers. We must begin with these simple agreements:

- We must evaluate our teachers. We must hold our teachers accountable for the successes and the failures of their students. We must continue to fine tune the evaluation system and stop the fighting. Teachers must be forced to move past the "how can you evaluate me, I teach children" curtain to the reality of "you must be evaluated, you teach children" truth. It does not matter what field you are in, teaching included, you have a right, a requirement, and a mandate that you too, just like everyone else working in the world today must be evaluated and held to that evaluation regarding future employment.

- We must begin to pay our teachers what they are worth. We cannot continue to expect, as a society, to have the best and the brightest entering a field that does not pay enough to support a family. We cannot expect that our teachers work a second job to make ends meet because their job is teaching and "after all they do it for the kids." If we want to attract the best to our field then we must pay for the best. Every great business or company knows that if you want the best, you seek them out, pay to get them, and continue to pay to keep them. Teaching must be no different. We must build our schools with the best regardless of their years of experience. We must bring the field of education to at least the current century and encourage teachers to change buildings and learn and grow. Regardless of who you are, teaching in the same building for year after year does not promote growth; it encourages stagnation. We cannot continue the practice of paying our teachers peanuts and "trapping" them in the same building because they cannot move anymore and expect better results from our schools.
- We must require ongoing, meaningful, research-based, current professional development in our schools for our teachers (and school leaders) every single year. We must support the time that it takes to do this and provide that to our teachers. We must allow there to be ongoing weekly (or minimally monthly) professional development both on-site and off. We must allow, and pay for, professional development from within the building as well as professional development from outside experts. We must, as stakeholders, demand that the very people educating and leading our schools are current on the most up-to-date learning styles, teaching methodology, data research, testing measures, and political mandates to run our classrooms and our schools. We cannot expect that our teachers not be trained and developed and expect our system to change.
- We must look at the day-to-day requirements and responsibilities we are putting on our teachers and our school administrators. We have to remember why we have them in the buildings in the first place. We must look at what they are doing, what we are asking them to do, and what is most important for them to do. We must look at what we should be valuing the most, teaching and learning, and look at ways to remove the "clutter" from the spinning and cracking plates of our teachers. We cannot expect to continue to "pile it on" and expect that it will not overflow to our students hampering their education.

WE HAVE GOT TO STOP THE GAMES IN STATE TESTING

I have not suggeested that testing itself should be eliminated. No educator would. No educator would suggest that their students should not be evaluated to measure their learning, and ultimately their teaching. That is not what is being said here at all. What is being said is this: we must stop the game of state testing. The games being spoken of are these:

- *The shell game*: Hiding the testing, the expectations, the curriculum, the standards, and the methodology of the test under various shells where we are all left guessing.
- *The telephone game*: The game where translation as to what we are testing, why we are testing, and when we are testing has become so lost that no one even remembers what the first test even was.
- *The mouse trap game*: The game of testing where the goal seems to be more like a "gotcha" rather than the real goal state testing was intended for, measuring teaching and learning.
- *The game of life*: The new game that now has the state test more of a measurement of success for our students than any other thing they do in school. It seems that success in a class, in a grade, with a teacher, on the field, or in any other manner in school is not relevant anymore and the only "measure" to a student's success and, for a large part our schools, has now become one state test. This state test has now manifested itself into measuring the "life" of our students in their educational journeys.
- *The game of poker*: This game is playing out in the political offices and politicians' platforms every day. It is a next move and ante up game that has schools as the chips in the center of the game being bet on. Testing companies and to some extent politicians are winning the pot on the backs of our students.
- *The game of chess*: Schools have become chess pieces in the state testing game. They have been forced to guess, manipulate, maneuver, and yes sometimes cheat and lie to attempt to beat this game. They are forever left to "guess" their opponent's next move and to react to the move that has been made.

Is playing these games what originally state testing was designed to do? No doubt they were not, but let me promise you this, we will gain no ground and will run our schools into the ground if we continue to test them to death. We will lose sight of all that we know our schools can and should be if all teachers do is prepare for, teach to, evaluate from, and live for the test. We must find the balance between what we test, when we test, and how often we test, together.

WE MUST TREAT EACH OTHER WITH DIGNITY AND RESPECT

Parents must begin to view their schools as partners rather than adversaries. We must work together, even through the difficult times, to do what is in the best interest of our students at all times. As parents, we must treat our teachers with respect. We must work together with our children's schools to assist, support, encourage, and never attack. No one gains and moves forward under attacks. We cannot expect the critical collaboration between a parent and their school to be an attack or a threat. We must treat that relationship as the nurturing, vital, and important relationship that it is.

OUR STUDENTS MUST BE HEARD AND THEIR OPINIONS VALUED

We have got to put students first and hear their voices. We have got to give them a voice in their education and stop forcing our beliefs and values on them. While a kindergarten student may not be able to articulate how they learn, a high school student can. We have to begin to hear their voices and stop shoving our version of school down their throats. They are intelligent human beings whose voices have been silenced in the decisions that have become school.

No one would ever begin to ask them because they "are just kids" and they "have no idea what they need." While we could agree that not every student would tell you what they hear or what they think is best, their voices must be heard and respected. When do the very students in our schools, the receivers of all of the rules, political grandstanding, state testing, and teacher evaluations and issues get a voice?

None of these suggestions are impossible. That is the truth. They are, though, at the very essence of what we must demand of our schools. If we continue to do what we have always done, then we will continue to get what we have always gotten. We all know that. We all know that in far too many ways the schools and classrooms of today are very similar to the schools and classrooms of yesterday, yet no one would argue that our students are different, our society is different, the careers are different, and the teachers are different, so much different, than yesterday.

How can we expect our students of today to learn in our world and our schools of yesterday? We can't and we must not! The intention of this book is to create conversations, great. It might even spark arguments, maybe heated ones, wonderful! But after the conversations and the arguments let's move forward with decisions, because, after all, our students, our teachers, and our administrators are waiting for those decisions.

Let this book be the beacon out in the darkness for so many who are just tired. They are in those classrooms and those schools each and every day doing their best to make a difference while others are attacking and arguing about what their next move will be. Let this book let them know that help is on the way and that they will be a part of that solution. Let this book be the light that shows us all to a new way in education. A way that is collaborative, kind, respectful, and full of trust in each other.

In closing let me say this: It has been an honor to have served the students, teachers, and stakeholders that have allowed me to teach, to lead, and to educate over the span of thirty years. If tomorrow were my last day on earth, I could be no more proud for the field that I entered, the field in which I spent thirty-plus years, the field from which I retired, and the field that offers me such pride to call my own . . . education.

To have walked with some amazing educators and have been in the presence of some amazing students bring immeasurable joy to my heart. We can make a difference, together. From this book, and what it will create is the next chapter of what is our part in education, because we all know that "The Education System is Broken," but together we can fix it! Teaching and making schools what we all know they can be. . . TOGETHER!